CREATIVE EVENTS FOR TRA

Creative events for trainers

Ken Jones

The McGraw-Hill Companies

London · New York · St Louis · San Francisco · Auckland
Bogotá · Caracas · Lisbon · Madrid · Mexico · Milan
Montreal · New Delhi · Panama · Paris · San Juan · São Paulo
Singapore · Sydney · Tokyo · Toronto

Published by
McGraw-Hill Publishing Company
Shoppenhangers Road, Maidenhead, Berkshire, SL6 2QL, England
Telephone: 01628 502500
Fax: 01628 770224

British Library Cataloguing in Publication Data

Jones, Ken,
   Creative events for trainers
   1. Employees – Traning of   2. Active learning
   I. Title
657.3'124'04
0-07-709-1930

Library of Congress Cataloging-in-Publication Data

Jones, Ken,
   Creative events for trainers / Ken Jones.
     p. cm.
   ISBN 0–07–709193–0 (pbk. : alk. paper)
   1. Management – Study and teaching – Simulation methods.
2. Executive – Training of.   I. Title.
HD30.4.J66   1997
658.4'07124–dc20   96–36160
                                                                                                                        CIP

McGraw-Hill
A Division of The McGraw·Hill Companies

Copyright © 1997 McGraw-Hill International (UK) Ltd. All rights reserved. Although this publication remains subject to copyright, permission is granted free of charge to photocopy the pages for instructional purposes which are required by each participant attending the training workshop. This may be done by the individual purchaser only. Under no circumstance will any reproduction of the designated materials or any portion thereof be either sold or distributed on a commercial basis. Except as expressly provided above, no part of this book may be reproduced or distributed in any form or by any means, or stored in a database or retrieval system, without the prior written permission of the publisher.

12345 CUP 9987

Typeset by Computape (Pickering) Ltd, North Yorkshire
Printed and bound in Great Britain at the University Press, Cambridge

Printed on Permanent Paper in compliance with ISO Standard 9706

Contents

Explanations   1
Introduction   3
Selecting the events—an overview   4
Selection by skills   6
Selection by subjects   10
Basic hints   13
Motives   15
Briefing   16
Action   19
Debriefing   21
Assessment   24

Events   27
1   Art work   29
2   Bad ideas   32
3   Ban, unban   36
4   Beyond beyond   40
5   Conference planning   46
6   Cracked pot   52
7   Creations   58
8   Cup and clip   61
9   Cutie Cat   65
10   Demotivate   69
11   Deoor Advertising   73
12   Games names   78
13   Guru training   82
14   I, Anxious   86
15   Island development   93
16   Jokes Inc.   97
17   Kissing campaign   101
18   Legislate   105
19   Lesser offspring   108
20   Lost Dreamers   113
21   Management poetry   118
22   Maze metaphor   122
23   Praise, blame   126
24   Pursuers, Pursued   132

25	Quality promotions	138
26	Rituals	143
27	Selling art	146
28	Skills alone	151
29	Sleeping Beauty	155
30	Spaceship Peace	159
31	Stupidity Bills	166
32	Television Kitchen	170
33	Training methods	174
34	Typists' veto	181
35	Virus X	187
36	War canoes	192
37	Year of the Dove	198

EXPLANATIONS

Introduction

Creative Events are designed to be thought-provoking. The scenarios are imaginative and the tasks are challenging. Those who participate in these events are invited to think creatively. Obeying instructions is not enough.

Any organization, no matter how routine its operations, is likely to benefit from creative thinking and, for any organization facing change, creative thinking is essential for efficiency and perhaps for survival.

There is one immediate and inevitable result of encouraging creative thinking—it is a conferment of value. It is an act which says that the person is a human being, not a cog. It is a statement of respect which benefits both those who encourage and those who receive the encouragement. Intrinsic in the use of any of these events is an invitation to a partnership of creative ideas. In itself it is a signal of open management.

Each event has its own notes for the facilitator. Each contains ideas for the briefing and debriefing and on how to organize the mechanics of the event. There are suggestions about numbers, groups and timing for that particular event. In addition, each event has a Briefing sheet for participants—which also helps the facilitator. There is a section on how to choose suitable events and how they might be graded, depending on the nature of the course, including the possibility of using an event as an icebreaker.

This book is not intended to replace direct instruction but to complement it. Any organization which values people should consider using such creative events as an integral part of training.

Selecting the events—an overview

There are two main ways of selecting individual events—by skills and by subjects. In addition, events could be selected in other ways—because they are brief or lengthy, or are icebreakers, or are easy to run. They could be selected because the language level required is easy, or the ethical values relate to the nature of the course, or because the behaviour is likely to be intellectual, artistic, competitive, caring, emotional or analytical.

Probably the essential characteristic of selection is that the event should be appropriate. The facilitator should be able to explain and defend the choice. And usually the explanation will relate in some way to the encouragement of creativity.

Skills These are listed in the grid relating to skills and are described on pages 6–8.

Subjects These are contained in the summary of the 37 events on pages (10–12) and also within each individual event.

Icebreakers These events are listed on page 9 in the grid relating to skills. They are also contained in the facilitator's notes for each icebreaker under the sub-heading 'Objectives'. The format of an icebreaker is for short person-to-person meetings, with each participant meeting as many other participants as possible. The length of time required increases with the number of participants.

Short events With a relatively small number of participants many of the events can be completed in an hour or less, particularly those with very little for the participants to read. A simple single-issue event is also likely to be relatively brief. Such events include Bad ideas, Rituals and Typists' veto. However, this is not to say that the value of such events would not be enhanced by extending the time-limits. Time is often a measure of the perceived importance of an event.

Long events Events with large numbers and/or relatively long documents are likely to take more than an hour. Events with a hidden agenda require time in the debriefing to reveal what was hidden (private information). There is also the question of the involvement of participants, the importance of the issues discussed, the elements of danger, organization and values. Events with potential for considerable discussion include Lost Dreamers, Sleeping Beauty, Spaceship Peace and Year of the Dove.

Easy for the facilitator Easy events have a simple structure, and the facilitator usually has no difficulty in relaxing and observing what happens. However, being easy for the facilitator does not necessarily mean that the events are easy for the participants. Some can be very challenging. The following events are particularly easy for the facilitator: Cracked pot, Games names, Virus X.

Selection by skills

The events in this book are all intended to:

- encourage creative thinking;
- give practice in the skills of artistry, communication, counselling, diplomacy, negotiation, planning, presentation, teamwork and time management;
- give confidence in thinking about, behaving in and coping with unusual situations;
- provide a wide variety of different situations, duties and ethical considerations;
- confer as much autonomy and responsibility as possible within the context of each event;
- provoke and amuse.

The following descriptions aim to clarify the categories of skill. The distinctions will be useful when choosing, running, debriefing and assessing the events.

Creativity This overall category for the book does not necessarily mean that participants will be creative, only that they have the opportunity to be creative. It requires imagination and a willingness to create as distinct from searching for precedents to hide behind and later, in the debriefing, justifying the behaviour by saying 'I only did what someone else did'.

Artistry This category is one of intention rather than accomplishment. Participants have the opportunity to be artistic either in creating a work of art or in appreciating artistic endeavour. No participant is told 'You must be an artist and draw/paint something'.

Communication By this is meant not what is communicated but how it is communicated—how people think, talk, listen and put forward ideas. It covers body language as well as spoken language and involves both common sense and logic. It is probably the broadest of the skill categories.

Counselling This is a situation in which people need help on a personal (albeit hypothetical) level from someone who can try to sympathize, understand and advise. It means active counselling, not simply planning to counsel.

Diplomacy The meaning does not relate to professional diplomacy as such, but is used instead in the sense in which one person might say to another, 'You could have been more diplomatic'. Diplomacy is usually a high-order skill, involving understanding other people's needs. It can be deceitful and it can be competitive, but it need be neither.

Negotiation Unlike diplomacy, negotiation necessarily involves bargaining. Usually what is at issue is fairly clear-cut, such as goods, services and money.

Planning Planning does not mean the plan itself, it means the behaviour of planning—the thoughts, concepts, objectives and actions of the people who plan.

Presentation By presentation is meant not just the final result but also the thoughts, the logic, the creativity and communication skills that go into the preparation. Presentation implies not only presenters but also an audience or a judging panel.

Teamwork The concept of teamwork covers group cooperation directed at objectives. It does not mean consensus at the expense of objectives. There is no value in participants being cooperative lemmings throwing themselves over a cliff. Teamwork can include objections, arguments, disputes, but it must involve a desire to work together. It can also involve setting up structures, dividing up tasks, accountability and checking.

Time management This means the behaviour of individuals or groups trying to organize a time schedule for tasks, as distinct from people simply getting on with the job as fast as they can.

Although not specifically skills, the final three categories—gender/race, hidden agenda and icebreakers—involve skill-related behaviour—sensitivity, diplomacy, tact, understanding, caring, etc.

Gender/race Although aspects of gender and race could arise in any educational activity, this category relates only to those events which necessarily (or probably) involve a consideration of gender and race. For example, the documents in Typists' veto make no mention of gender or race, but if the participants envisage that the lower paid staff of an imaginary company are mainly female and/or from ethnic minorities, then the event will involve aspects of gender and race.

Hidden agenda In the context of this book, a hidden agenda means that some information is private. Whether the participants concerned decide to keep the information secret or share it with other participants is a question for them to decide in the light of their functions, duties and responsibilities.

Icebreakers The format of these icebreakers is to provide an opportunity for each participant to meet—face-to-face—as many other participants as reasonably possible in the time available. Icebreakers are suitable not only at the beginning of courses or conferences but at any point when 'ice' has formed—when there are frosty silences or when the participants have frozen themselves into groups based on gender or race or job or friendships or cliques. An icebreaker is not the same thing as a friendship session—participants have to take account of their functions, duties and responsibilities.

No.	Title	creativity	artistry	communication	counselling	diplomacy	negotiation	planning	presentation	teamwork	time management	gender/race	hidden agenda	icebreaker
1	Art work	✓	✓	✓				✓	✓	✓	✓			
2	Bad ideas	✓		✓						✓				✓
3	Ban, unban	✓		✓				✓		✓	✓			✓
4	Beyond beyond	✓		✓	✓	✓	✓	✓						
5	Conference planning	✓		✓				✓	✓	✓	✓		✓	
6	Cracked pot	✓		✓		✓		✓		✓	✓			
7	Creations	✓	✓	✓		✓		✓	✓	✓	✓			
8	Cup and clip	✓		✓	✓	✓					✓			✓
9	Cutie Cat	✓		✓				✓	✓	✓	✓			
10	Demotivate	✓		✓		✓		✓		✓	✓			
11	Deoor advertising	✓	✓	✓				✓	✓	✓	✓			
12	Games names	✓		✓		✓	✓	✓		✓				✓
13	Guru training	✓		✓				✓	✓	✓				✓
14	I, Anxious	✓		✓	✓					✓	✓	✓		
15	Island development	✓		✓				✓	✓	✓	✓			
16	Jokes Inc.	✓	✓	✓		✓		✓		✓	✓			
17	Kissing campaign	✓		✓		✓	✓			✓	✓	✓		✓
18	Legislate	✓		✓		✓	✓	✓	✓	✓	✓			
19	Lesser offspring	✓		✓	✓	✓		✓						
20	Lost Dreamers	✓		✓		✓		✓	✓	✓		✓	✓	
21	Management poetry	✓	✓	✓				✓	✓	✓	✓			
22	Maze metaphor	✓	✓	✓	✓			✓	✓	✓	✓			
23	Praise, blame	✓		✓		✓				✓	✓			✓
24	Pursuers, Pursued	✓		✓		✓	✓	✓		✓				
25	Quality promotions	✓		✓				✓	✓	✓	✓			
26	Rituals	✓		✓		✓					✓			✓
27	Selling art	✓	✓	✓		✓	✓	✓	✓	✓	✓			
28	Skills alone	✓		✓		✓				✓				
29	Sleeping Beauty	✓		✓		✓	✓	✓		✓				
30	Spaceship Peace	✓		✓		✓	✓	✓	✓	✓	✓	✓	✓	
31	Stupidity bills	✓		✓			✓	✓	✓	✓				
32	Television Kitchen	✓		✓				✓	✓	✓				
33	Training methods	✓		✓	✓				✓	✓				
34	Typists' veto	✓		✓	✓			✓		✓		✓		
35	Virux X	✓		✓				✓		✓	✓			
36	War canoes	✓		✓		✓	✓	✓	✓			✓	✓	
37	Year of the Dove	✓	✓	✓		✓	✓	✓	✓	✓		✓	✓	

Selection by subjects

Art work	A simulation about a company intending to use art and artistry in routine jobs.
Bad ideas	In which executives start with bad ideas in order to create good ideas.
Ban, unban	About a new political party proposing to ban something, or unban it.
Beyond beyond	Consultants meet clients who seek experiences beyond beyond.
Conference planning	About planning the timetable and contents of a conference.
Cracked pot	Dealing with the media which has an embarrassing story about the company.
Creations	Designing fashions involving the theme of the theatre.
Cup and clip	Dealing with job stress as represented by a cup and a paper clip.
Cutie Cat	A debt recovery company plans to use embarrassment.
Demotivate	In which consultants create plans to demotivate staff.
Deoor advertising	The advertising of a product named Deoor—or any anagram of that name.
Games names	A developing country seeks more appropriate names for well-known games.

Guru training	About planning and advertising a course for training management gurus.
I, Anxious	The house magazine of a large company seeks assistant editors for an 'Anxious' page.
Island development	Tobacco company executives plan to buy and use an island.
Jokes Inc.	Authors and publishers plan to produce humorous books.
Kissing campaign	A glossy magazine plans a campaign for courteous gestures to replace doffing the hat.
Legislate	Members of Parliament try to put their election aims into legislative language.
Lesser offspring	Consultants are visited by the sons and daughters of famous parents.
Lost Dreamers	Explorers visit a long-lost Dreamers' tribe.
Management poetry	About a magazine running a competition for poems about management.
Maze metaphor	The counselling service of a large company devises a scheme involving a maze.
Praise, blame	A meeting of management, staff and customers of a travel agency.
Pursuers, Pursued	In which the staff at a television company are pursuers or pursued.
Quality promotions	Planning to grade staff by numbers to indicate quality and potential for promotion.
Rituals	About devising and using rituals for meetings.

Selling art	Artists, gallery owners and art magazines deal with new works of art.
Skills alone	Involving job interviews relating to qualities rather than specific jobs.
Sleeping Beauty	In which Sleeping Beauty, the Prince, the King, the Queen and the Witch meet scribes and lawyers.
Spaceship Peace	A spaceship for peace runs out of food and visits Earth.
Stupidity Bills	In which Members of Parliament seek to legislate against stupidity.
Television Kitchen	A television station and groups of cookery school staff.
Training methods	About devising plans for assessing and improving training.
Typists' veto	Involving plans to give typists the power of veto on letters and documents.
Virus X	About an isolated group trying to survive a natural disaster.
War canoes	About a tribe which has sighted war canoes in the distance.
Year of the Dove	Scribes of the Mountains meet scribes of the Plains to exchange information and ideas.

Basic hints

If you are not experienced in running interactive events it is easy to assume that reading the documents will enable you to predict what is likely to happen. But unlike a poem (novel, textbook) a simulation does not exist in the documents. A simulation is action—the actions (thoughts, motives, behaviour) of the participants. Therefore it requires experience of how participants react when given power, duties and responsibilities in order to predict what is likely to happen.

It is quite normal for teachers and trainers who are not familiar with simulations to look at the documents and decide that the event is too difficult for the participants. They may think, 'But what are the participants supposed to do?' Very often there are no specific instructions to participants—only functions, duties and obligations relating to a specific environment. Negative judgements about participants' ability to cope often fail to take into account (a) the abilities of the participants when given authority and (b) the extent to which participants help each other.

It is important to understand the nature of the methodology—the aims, the methods. The documents are not there to be learned, they are there to be used. The participants are not the same as trainees or students. Participants, by the nature of their roles, are not under tuition or training. They 'own' the events, and it is up to them to take decisions and responsibility for their actions in the light of the situation. Professional expertise is not required, but professional involvement is.

The best way to understand what is involved is to explore the event from the inside rather than the outside—to look at it from the point of view of the participant, not the facilitator. There are two fairly easy ways of doing this. One is to use imagination. You are a business executive (artist, reporter, lawyer, king, alien) and you are aware of the situation and your duties. Turning to another participant who is in role X, you say—what? What are the actual words in direct speech, not reported speech? Now imagine that you are the other participant—how do you respond to the remark? And so on—changing roles (functions) and allowing your imagination to develop the potential for action.

The second way is to run the event with a few friends (family, colleagues). It can be a shortened and simplified version, but it should be for real. The guinea pigs should be inside the event. For example, they should say, 'I think we should draw up an agenda' and not, 'If I were in this situation I would say "I think we should draw up an agenda"'.

In both the personal imagination route and the guinea pig route the key question is not, 'What are the participants learning and have they got the right answer?' but, 'How are they behaving? What are they thinking? What skills are they using?' The debriefing sections in the facilitator's notes contain some of the questions that can be asked about the participants' thoughts, skills, motives, feelings, behaviour.

The main hazard in running any interactive event is using inappropriate terminology which could lead to inappropriate behaviour. For example, to advertise a forthcoming event as a game is fine if the event is a game, but not if it is intended to be another methodology. Even experienced facilitators often come unstuck because they see no differences between games, simulations, exercises and role-plays. They think of the labels as nouns, not verbs and fail to see that psychologically the four methodologies are different, distinctive and incompatible. 'Stop playing games' is a real-life admonition—an accusation of inappropriate behaviour. The consequences of some participants being in a gaming mode while others are in the simulation mode or are play-acting or treating it as an exercise can range from mildly irritating to horrendously traumatic. (For examples of what can go wrong, see the chapter 'Ambivalents' in my book *Simulations. A Handbook for Teachers and Trainers*, Kogan Page, 1995.)

If there is any likelihood that any participant may be in a different methodology from the other participants, photocopy and hand out, the following page on MOTIVES. Quite apart from helping to avoid incompatible methodologies during the action, the page is useful as a tool of analysis in the debriefing.

Motives

The two methodologies—games and simulations—are psychologically incompatible. The motives are distinctive, separate, conflicting and irreconcilable.

In a game the participants think of themselves as players and the aim (motive, duty) is to try to win. In a simulation the motive is to accept one's role (function) and behave 'professionally' in the context of real-world ethics, real-world duties and responsibilities. For example, in the debriefing a facilitator might ask,' 'Why did you knock down houses and build hotels?' If it were a game the reply might be, 'Because I wanted to win'. If it were a simulation the reply might be, 'Well, I was concerned about making people homeless, but I planned to set aside some of my profits to help rehouse them'.

Participants can be hurt and friendships broken if some participants are in the gaming mode while others are in the simulation mode. So it is important to distinguish between the two modes in order that the event is psychologically consistent. It is also useful to distinguish between role-plays and exercises as these also can produce conflicting behaviours.

Simulations Expertise is not required. The motive of participants is to do their best in the situations in which they find themselves and accept the duties and responsibilities of their roles. The motives are 'professional' and involve real-world ethics and conventions. Participants keep their own personalities; they do not play-act a role (function). If a participant has a role of executive, that person is an executive by virtue of taking decisions.

Games The implicit and essential motive in all games of skill is that players should try to win. If participants do not try to win they are not players in a game but are fun-lovers in a pastime, or possibly they are using the event as a training session. Games have no real-world ethics, except in the concept of fair play. Knocking down houses to build hotels cannot be unethical because there is no code of law or ethics, only the rules of the game which provide a self-contained magic kingdom.

Role-play The word 'play' is significant and suggests that the motive is play-acting (imitating, mimicking, performing). For example, if the role is 'king' and the participant imitates George III, then the behaviour is role-play. If, however, the participant accepted the function of king and was motivated by the duties and responsibilities of monarchy, then the behaviour would be in the simulation mode.

Exercises In the context of learning it is useful to think of an exercise as a problem-solving situation. The motive is to solve the problem and the only role is that of a problem solver. The participants remain themselves—students, trainees, learners.

Briefing

The briefing is essentially the initial period to establish the mechanics of the event—to discuss any time-limits, the facilities available and who sits (or stands) where.

Do not use the briefing to give advice on matters of substance or to discuss matters of substance. Do not say, 'I advise you to draw up an agenda', or, 'Look at all the options before you do anything else', or, 'Ask me if you have any difficulties'. In the briefing distinguish between the mechanics ('Where do we sit and what is the time-limit?') and questions of substance ('Are we to discuss whether the media might be interested in our plans?'). To questions of substance it can be useful to say, 'I'm not here' or, 'I'm not an executive in your company'.

Regarding the allocation of roles (functions, duties) it is advisable to do this at random. If participants are allowed to pick their own roles, some might feel that the 'best' roles went to the most pushy. If you allocate the roles, some participants might think you were prejudiced or unfair. It is true that randomness will break up friendship groups and cliques, but that can be justified on several grounds—for example, 'We cannot always pick and choose our roles in real life', 'Randomness helps you to get to know other people', 'Randomness proves that you are not being manipulated; everyone has the same chance'.

One argument against randomness is that real-life experts may not get the roles that are appropriate to their skills and the result will fall short of excellence. This is a mistaken objection since the aim is not excellence, it is to provide opportunities for creativity and other skills. To try to enhance the 'result' by choosing the most able participants for the most important roles is in conflict with the philosophy of these events.

Briefing sheets

There is a temptation for the facilitator not to bother making copies of the Briefing sheets, but merely to summarize what it says. This can work, but it is a dangerous short cut because the Briefing sheets

- provide an insurance against forgetting to mention a key point and having to interrupt the action later to say, 'Sorry, I should have told you that ...';
- help in avoiding an overbriefing, of saying too much, of telling the participants what decisions to take, of dropping hints, guiding them and generally undermining their authority as decision makers.

The Briefing sheets simply set the scene and mention the procedures. They should be retrieved before the action starts because they are not documents inside the action—as are the memos, forms, letters, lists, identity cards. By removing the 'Briefing' documents the decks are cleared for the reality—the event itself. The removal helps to emphasize the vital point of the methodology—that the participants are in professional roles and are not trainees or students under instruction.

Authenticity

Before running any event, consider whether any reasonable and appropriate steps can be taken to increase the authenticity of the occasion. This depends entirely on the hypothetical working environment. It could be an office or an art gallery or a television studio or an abandoned schoolroom.

What should always be done is to remove any personal clutter that is inappropriate—coats, briefcases, umbrellas, timetables and all non-relevant documents. Usually these objects can be placed on a side table.

Little touches can often make a big difference. An event that envisages a coffee break can be enhanced by having refreshments delivered to the room. A boardroom environment can be enhanced by pens and notepads and perhaps glasses and a carafe of water. However, avoid trying to introduce so much authenticity that it becomes a distraction. As mentioned above, authenticity is always helped by retrieving all the Briefing sheets before the action begins.

An essential consideration is the furniture and the layout of the room. For example, all icebreakers envisage people standing up and moving around, so if an icebreaker is run in a lounge with deep armchairs some special arrangements will be needed to ensure a flow of traffic. Some events require changes in the furniture halfway through. For example, the first stage may envisage widely separated groups, whereas the next stage could involve one team engaged in a presentation and all the other teams being a single audience. If the facilitator leaves the participants in their original groups and asks them to turn round to look at the presentation, the message received by the participants could be that the facilitator does not have a high opinion of either the event or themselves.

Some events require privacy, so it is useful to look at ways of achieving this. Groups might move out into the corridor or another room. A refreshment break in the snack bar could be used for private discussions.

The advantages of considering the question of authenticity are not limited to the plausibility of the environment. Your efforts could produce a glow of satisfaction from participants when they realize that they and the event are being treated with seriousness, consideration and imagination. This in turn can boost their feelings of autonomy and enhance their decision-making powers.

Documents

All the events in this book require facsimile documents—memos, forms, letters, etc. Sometimes each participant should have a copy of a document, sometimes only one copy is required for each group or team.

There is an appropriate time for handing out documents. The facsimile documents are appropriate to the action but not to the briefing. Therefore they should be handed out at the start of the action and not during the briefing. Similarly, the Briefing sheets are appropriate only in the briefing and should be retrieved at the end of the briefing and before the facsimile documents are handed out.

Scrap paper can be thought of as a potential facsimile document. It is often useful and sometimes a necessary tool. It can become an agenda, chart, design, or even a doodle. Other types of documents can be produced on overhead projectors, video, tape recorders, computers, flipcharts, etc.

Some events have optional roles depending on numbers—for example, a management team to judge presentations. If this is the case, it is important that the management team has the facsimile documents that it would have in such a situation—its own memos, forms, etc. There is also the question of appropriate facilities for a management team, which can be discussed in the briefing, and the facilitator should explore the options before running the event.

It is surprising that facilitators sometimes get into a muddle over documents—by not running off copies of a document or running off too many or too few. This can have serious consequences in an interactive event if the mistake is noticed only after the action has begun. Not only is it embarrassing to say, 'Sorry, I forgot to run off copies of the memo from your boss, I'll be back with some in a minute', but it also causes participants to come out of role, reduces their involvement and damages the authenticity. A last-minute check of the documents is always advisable.

Action

When running the events, the most important objective for a facilitator is invisibility. Unfortunately, the habits of instruction can make this a difficult objective to achieve. It is all too easy for a facilitator to enter the boardroom and ask the executives whether they have understood what they are supposed to do, whether they have considered drawing up an agenda, whether they realize that it is a good idea to read between the lines of the document they have just been given, etc.

The motives for trying to usurp participant autonomy are usually:

1 The habit of instruction.
2 A genuine desire to improve the result.
3 A defensive measure to prevent things going 'wrong'.

Intervention is inconsistent with the methodology. Participant autonomy is essential in these events; otherwise they become guided exercises or training sessions or tuition periods. The participants must be allowed the freedom of professionals, and that includes the freedom to make mistakes.

It is a good idea to reconcile oneself to the view that disasters, although not desirable, are excellent ways of learning and to remember that each event is followed by a debriefing in which lessons can be drawn from what occurred. It follows from this that facilitators should intervene only on questions of mechanics and procedure: 'May we give a news conference?', 'May we have another 10 minutes?', 'Can we use the overhead projector?' If, however, the questions are to do with policy or substance ('Do you want us to support this proposal?' or 'Are we allowed to draw up an agenda?'), then avoid giving a straight answer. As mentioned earlier in the section on briefing, the best reply is probably (a) you are not there or (b) you are not on the staff of the organization.

However, intervention is required if a participant opts out of an event, and it is worth while for the facilitator to draw up one or two contingency plans that take into account the nature of the course and the sort of participants who are involved.

The general advice given for such situations is to start by finding out what has gone wrong. It may have nothing to do with the event itself and may be purely personal. One way of dealing with it is to use the simulated environment of the event itself, perhaps sending a message to the participant that there is a telephone call from the Managing Director, the Editor, the King or whatever role is plausible. Once the participant is withdrawn from the event it is usually fairly easy to see whether the objection is fundamental or something based on a trivial misunderstanding. If it is fundamental, then it is probably best not to argue or try to persuade the participant to continue, but to accept the decision without demur and offer alternatives. Ask whether the participant would be willing to continue in a different role or in a different group. If neither suggestion is accepted, then you could suggest that the participant might like to continue as an observer or a deputy facilitator.

All the events are flexible regarding timing and numbers. One can give only a rough generalization unless one knows the circumstances—the type of course, the experience of participants, the facilitator's attitude to debriefing and so on. So the times given in the introductions to the events should be regarded as approximations. The best way to obtain more concrete evidence is to do a trial run. The same dependence on circumstances applies to the number of participants. The procedures are flexible. Two participants could share one role or one participant could take on two roles, for example. Also, with large numbers the same event could be run in parallel groups simultaneously.

Debriefing

It is not uncommon for facilitators to feel less confident about handling the debriefing of a simulation, exercise or game than they do about running the event. Perhaps because of a lack of confidence, facilitators sometimes allow an event to overrun and the debriefing is either shortened or even omitted. In general, debriefings tend to be unimaginative. It is commonly assumed that a debriefing must consist of the facilitator asking questions and drawing conclusions. Occasionally it can take the form of a lecture in which the facilitator tells the participants what they have learned. As this book is about creative events, it is appropriate to try to make the debriefing as creative as possible within the bounds of what is appropriate.

The question of how the debriefing is handled depends on the facilitator's attitudes—whether it is preferable to be in charge or to hand over at least some of the responsibility to the participants; whether to run a routine and safe debriefing or whether to be innovative.

Some options

Here is a list of a few of the possibilities, so that you can sort out which options you favour most, which ideas you are familiar with and which procedures you are willing to try—at least as a one-off experiment.

- Allowing a committee of participants to run the debriefing, having warned them about this in advance of the event.
- Using small group debriefings, at least as a starting point.
- Using the format of a public opinion poll, with each participant being given a clipboard on which he or she writes his or her own question(s) and has to obtain as many answers as possible by individually interviewing other people.
- Giving responsibility to sub-committees to investigate the behaviour that occurred—the private thoughts as well as the public utterances, the rejected ideas as well as those made public.
- Deferring the debriefing for an hour or day or week in order to allow more considered (and perhaps less emotional) views to emerge.
- Negotiating with the participants the form of the debriefing in advance of the event itself.

The aims of the debriefing should be considered before running the event, as the aims are likely to influence what you look for specifically during the event itself.

If you are running an event for the first time, you could concentrate on those areas, particularly areas of creativity and skills, that are mentioned in the sections on debriefing the particular event. These ideas are based on previous experiences of running the events in a variety of situations. For example, starting points during the action are particularly well worth observing in relation to skills. Do the participants immediately pick up their pens as if they were diligent hermits, or do they talk, discuss and examine options? Do they try to manage time or do they adopt an immediate hands-on approach and later complain that you did not give them enough time to complete the task? How do they deal with difficulties and disagreements?

The more familiar you are with an event, the easier you will find the task of observing, assessing and debriefing.

You could opt for a structured approach by drawing up a checklist of objectives and preparing self-assessment sheets. The advantage is that it links the results with the objectives. The participants can see for themselves how they have got on. The relevance becomes self-evident. The participants can satisfy themselves about the reasons for participating in the event within the context of the objectives of the course. From this it is only a short step to discovering what they have gained from the experience. The disadvantage of a structured approach is that it tends to ignore or overlook some of the most interesting and relevant events that occurred but were not predicted. Such unusual or innovative episodes, including disasters, are often the most memorable features; they are the building blocks for learning from experience.

The debriefing may also deal with the relevance of the scenario. For example, in Spaceship Peace someone may say that it is fantasy and not real life. This could lead to a discussion about what was real in the event. How real were the thoughts, the emotions, the motives, the planning, the diplomacy? In creative events the relevance lies mainly in the skills, including the skills of dealing with the unusual. The unusual is important because it provides a level playing field. The participants are denied the textbook answers. What matters is the participants themselves.

If the debriefing moves into the field of discussing the educational value of the event, the combination of creative thinking and unusual situations could elicit some of the following points:

1 It allows participants to escape the constraints of habit and stereotyped thinking.
2 It promotes equality of opportunity, as distinct from a hierarchy of experts or domination by gender or race.
3 It encourages human interaction, understanding and cooperation.
4 It facilitates innovation and experiment because creativity, not excellence, is the main aim.

Explanations

5 It enables principles to be examined without the clutter and complexity of real-world institutions.
6 It helps the facilitator and participants to assess human qualities, as distinct from fact-learning.

The objective of encouraging creative thinking is not so much to produce bright ideas as to widen the horizons of behaviour.

Assessment

It is worth noting that assessment is inevitable, even if there is no debriefing. Participants and facilitators cannot avoid thinking about what happened in the events and they naturally evaluate what occurred according to their normal values—educational, social and ethical. By far the greatest part of such assessments are unnoticed, occurring in private chats in the coffee bar or staff room or just meditated upon privately. Such reflections and assessments can occur and recur days, weeks or even years after the events themselves.

'I never thought I (he/she) could do that' is not an uncommon experience. If participant A finds that participant B has creativity (integrity, wit, compassion, shrewdness, tact, eloquence, attentiveness, loyalty) this can be significant, valuable and can shape lives and friendships—quite irrespective of the facilitator's assessment of the event itself.

There are two quite different aims and methods of assessment. One is to assess the event itself and the other is to assess the participants.

The event

Assessing the event will presumably be a comparison of events used for specific purposes. The question might be: 'With these particular trainees/students on this particular course and devoting this amount of time to the event, have the objectives been better achieved with event A or B?'

There have been studies which have sought to achieve global answers about events based on questionnaires: 'How useful did you find it?', 'Did it help develop communication skills?', 'Did you learn what it is like to be a disadvantaged person?' The problem with such global answers is that circumstances are so varied that the answers are local rather than global. Nevertheless, experience of running events does enable one to say such things as, 'Event A is preferable to Event B because it is consistent in its methodology, because it is elegant, interesting and well balanced, because the documents are well written and because it arouses more discussion in the debriefing'.

The participants

Assessing the participants requires judgements different from those for assessing the event. If the course is designed to assess skills, this can be done formally, with a structured list based on the objectives listed for each event. The assessment can include (a) the facilitator's assessment of the participants, (b) each participant's assessment of other participants and (c) each participant's assessment of himself or herself. Various categories could be used: for example, poor, fair, good and excellent. Some overall assessment may also be useful.

Obviously, tests for behaviour are not like tests for the recall of information. Not only are they more subjective, they often involve group work, whereas memory tests are solitary experiences. It is also a matter of values. In the everyday world, human values and human qualities, subjective though they are, have considerable importance. It is a mistake to be dismissive about human behaviour on the grounds that it is subjective. It is because it is subjective that it is so valuable.

Assessment of incidents can be just as valuable as assessment of skills. Those involved in the incidents are the experts. They and they alone know their own motives and emotions. What observers may see can be misleading or misunderstood. The lessons learned from assessing incidents can also be more easily applied than receiving a mark for skills. The incidents examined should not be limited to mistakes or disasters—looking at effective behaviour is also illuminating.

The events in this book cover a wide range of opportunities for creativity, for skills, for behaviour. When chosen appropriately, they create and provoke a wealth of experiences—raw material for learning from experience.

EVENTS

1 Art work

Description A simulation about a company intending to use art and artistry in routine jobs.

Objectives To enhance the skills of creativity, artistry, communication, planning, presentation, teamwork and time management.

Time and numbers With small numbers the event might last for an hour, but with larger numbers allow up to two hours. The minimum number is probably six. There is no maximum number. With a dozen or more participants one or two could be given the role of management and take on the job of organizing and judging the presentations.

Resources
- Briefing sheet—one copy for each participant.
- Memo—one copy for each participant.
- Scrap paper—and possibly large sheets for the presentations.
- Presentation facilities—possibly overhead projector, flipchart, etc.

Method
1 Hand out the Briefing sheets—one copy for each participant. Discuss the facilities and set a time-limit for the beginning of the presentations.
2 Retrieve all the Briefing sheets and divide the participants (preferably at random) into teams of between two and five. If there are sufficient numbers choose one team (at random) to represent management.
3 Hand out the Memo—one copy for each participant. Make available the scrap paper and other facilities.
4 If there is a management team it can take charge of arranging the presentations—probably rearranging the furniture and giving each team a number to show the order of presentation.

Debriefing It could be useful to begin by teams debriefing themselves—mainly to discuss their views of the various presentations, including their own. The subsequent general discussion could begin with what the participants do not know—the ideas that were rejected by the other teams. Probably the debriefing will concentrate on the skills involved in creating artistic ideas, communication, teamwork, the planning and presentations, plus the question of time management.

Briefing

This is a simulation about a company—Alpha Furniture Suppliers—intending to use art and artistry in routine jobs. You are in the role of a member of the staff. Do not invent your own hypothetical job—it is irrelevant. Do not invent 'facts' to win an argument: 'The packers have told me they all want taped classical music'.

The first part of the event is the creation of artistic ideas and the second part is the presentation of these ideas. You will receive a Memo explaining the situation, plus scrap paper.

Alpha Furniture Supplies

MEMO

From: Board of Management

To: All staff

We want your ideas about using art and artistry to enliven and enhance job satisfaction in our three departments—Office, Saleroom and Warehouse.

The ideas must include an ingredient of art—even if it is only taped music. However, we hope your plans will be more ambitious, particularly for those jobs which are repetitious—packing, loading, stock-taking, invoicing, etc. Your aim should be to arouse the soul, to infuse artistry. However, we do not wish to put ideas into your heads. It is for you to put ideas into our heads.

Each team must make a presentation. Try to involve all members of your team in the presentation. We will consider your ideas very carefully. By next month we hope to reward all teams which produced good ideas, and those teams which produce good presentations will be appraised for possible career advancement.

Please note: there will be a strict deadline. Decide on the presentation before the deadline—decide who should do what. We shall not be overjoyed if we observe any team, or any member of any team, working on ideas after the deadline. To avoid temptation, we advise teams to split up while watching other presentations.

2 Bad ideas

Description A simulation in which executives start with bad ideas in order to create good ideas.

Objectives To enhance the skills of creativity, communication and time management and can be used as an icebreaker.

Time and numbers With small numbers, the event might last for an hour. If there are large numbers, more time will be needed in the debriefing for explanations and comparisons and the event could take up to two hours. The minimum number is probably eight. There is no maximum number.

Resources
- Briefing sheet—one copy for each participant.
- Memo—one copy for each participant.
- Bad ideas form—one copy for each participant.
- Scrap paper.

Method
1. Hand out the Briefing sheets—one copy for each participant. Set a time-limit for the end of the action—allowing sufficient time for as many participants as possible to meet each other face-to-face.
2. Retrieve all the Briefing sheets. Hand out the Memo and the Bad ideas form—one copy of each for each participant. Make scrap paper available and allow at least five minutes for participants to devise their bad ideas.

Debriefing It could be useful to begin by asking the final pairs to debrief themselves—mainly to form their views of the progress of their own bad ideas. The subsequent general discussion could cover the skills involved in creating bad ideas and improving on them, on creativity, communication and time management. If the event was used as an icebreaker it can be worth while to discuss how well it worked in this respect.

Briefing

This is a simulation in which executives in Alpha Management Advice Company individually create a bad idea, then divide into pairs which meet briefly to modify and improve the ideas. The pairs then split up and new pairs form.

The situation is explained in a Memo from the Managing Director, and it can be assumed from the Memo that one or more of the directors would be present to keep an eye on things.

Alpha Management Advice Company

MEMO

From: Managing Director

To: All Executives

Our consultancy has performed significantly worse than most of our rivals. This is partly due to laziness in searching for options. It seems that our staff have simply put forward the first 'good' idea that occurred to them.

This 'jumping to judgement' could easily become a habit, and the Board has decided to set up an 'exploration study';

(a) to encourage creativity, widen horizons and expand adoptions, and
(b) to see if bad ideas can lead to good ideas.

Individually and without consulting anyone, devise a bad idea for management and write it on your Bad Ideas form. It must relate to one (only) of the following:

1   Management of the public libraries in a city.
2   Management of a national opera house which puts on opera and ballet.
3   Management of a chain of shops selling cosmetics.

If you cannot think of a bad idea, then write: 'Opera House—the performers to decide on budgets'.

The bad idea should be bad but not ludicrous or comic. It should have a degree of plausibility. Without consulting anyone, mark one of the boxes at the top of your Bad Ideas form and write your idea (briefly). Then meet in pairs and write modifications of the other person's idea on the other person's form. Do not spend too long with one person—try to meet everyone. Manage your time well.

Finally, at the end of the meetings, add your own comment or modifications at the bottom of your own form. We look forward to seeing the development of ideas.

Alpha Management Advice Company

Name ....

Tick idea area (one box only)   libraries ☐   opera house ☐   shops ☐

My bad idea is ....

....

....

Names	Comments and/or modifications

3 Ban, unban

Description A simulation about a new political party proposing to ban something, or unban it.

Objectives To enhance the skills of creativity, communication, planning, teamwork and time management and can be used as an icebreaker.

Time and numbers With small numbers, the event might last for an hour. If there are large numbers, more time will be needed in the debriefing for explanations and comparisons and the event could take up to two hours. The minimum number is probably eight. There is no maximum number.

Resources
- Briefing sheet—one copy for each participant.
- Letter—one copy for each participant.
- Ban/Unban form—one copy for each participant.
- Scrap paper.

Method
1. Hand out the Briefing sheets—one to each participant—and discuss the facilities. The event has two parts—discussions in pairs followed by a general meeting and this is likely to require rearranging the furniture.
2. Set two time-limits—one for the end of the meetings of pairs and the other for the end of the general meeting.
3. Retrieve the Briefing sheets.
4. Hand out the Letter and the Ban/Unban form—one of each for each participant. Make scrap paper available.

Debriefing It could be useful to begin by taking it in turns to reveal the ideas that were abandoned or amended. The subsequent general discussion could cover the skills involved. How sensitive were participants in dealing with other people's ideas, bearing in mind that they were all in the same Party? Was there any negotiation—'We will support your idea if you support ours'? How well did the general meeting organize itself? Was it democratic? If the event was used as an icebreaker, how well did it work?

Briefing

This is a simulation about a new political party in the Republic of Alpha—the Expedient Party. The Party believes that many people in Alpha are dissatisfied with the confrontational politics of the two main parties. The Expedient Party wants issues decided on their merits and not by party dogmas.

The Expedient Party wants to ban things, or unban them, on the issues involved—justice, ethics, economics and so on. The Party has no ideology, but it is committed to fairness, caring and democracy. Because it believes in democracy it has decided to consult all its members by holding small meetings throughout the country to put forward ideas about what might be banned, or unbanned.

You are a member of the Expedient Party and will be taking part in one of these local meetings. You will have a letter from the Party's headquarters explaining the situation. You will also have a Ban/Unban form on which you write your own idea, and it has space for other members to add their comments.

In creating your ideas about what might be banned or unbanned you can assume that the laws and regulations of Alpha are virtually the same as the laws and regulations that govern you.

The Expedient Party
the party of ideas, not dogmas

Dear Local Members,

Thank you for your support in the democratic process of forming proposals for our Party. We hope your meeting will be pleasant and useful.

Please begin by working as individuals. Write on your Ban/Unban form something that you think might be banned or unbanned. Do not consult with anyone. If you cannot think of an idea, write down nothing—ideas will occur to you later when you meet other members.

Then meet face-to-face with another member and write comments about the idea on each other's form. Keep the meeting brief and move on to meet someone else. Try to meet everyone. After the meetings in pairs, form into a general discussion group and try to agree on at least one idea to put up to national level. How you organize this meeting is up to you.

Best wishes,

President and Committee
National Headquarters

The Expedient Party
the party of ideas, not dogmas

Name:

One thing which should be banned (unbanned) is: _____

_____

_____

Brief comments on this idea by other members:

Names   Comments

4 Beyond beyond

Description A simulation in which consultants meet clients who seek experiences beyond beyond.

Objectives To enhance the skills of creativity, communication, counselling, diplomacy, negotiation and planning.

Time and numbers With small numbers, the event might last for an hour. If there are large numbers, more time will be needed in the debriefing for explanations and comparisons and the event could take up to two hours. The minimum number is probably eight. There is no maximum number.

Resources
- Briefing sheet—one copy for each participant.
- Advertisement form—one copy for each consultancy.
- Standard Contract—several copies for each consultancy.
- My Diary Notes—one copy for each client.
- Signalling device (bell, buzzer, whistle, banging the table).

Method *Note:* Because the concept 'beyond beyond' is vague it may be advisable not to choose this simulation as the first creative event to run.

1. Hand out the Briefing sheets—one copy for each participant.
2. Divide the participants, preferably at random, so that there is roughly the same number of clients as there are consultancies. If one or two participants might need help they could be placed on the staff of a consultancy rather than have the role of an individual client. Or two participants could share the role of one client (both being the same hypothetical person) and help each other.
3. Set an overall time-limit for the action. Set a time-limit for each consultation—at least three minutes—as without a time-limit some participants may be sitting around and becoming dissatisfied. Explain that you will give a signal for meetings to break up.
4. Arrange the furniture to ensure that each meeting is as private as possible. Discuss how the advertisements will be publicized—perhaps placed on a board.
5. Retrieve all the Briefing sheets.

6 Hand out the Advertisement form—one copy to each consultancy. Hand out several copies of the Standard Contract to the consultancies. Hand out My Diary Notes—one copy for each client.
7 During the action signal the times for clients to move to other consultancies.

Debriefing

Since participants will not know what went on during other consultations it could be a good idea to start with everyone taking it in turns to give a brief but factual (and non-argumentative) account of what occurred. The subsequent discussion will probably cover areas of skills, but might also venture into questions of metaphysics (beyond physics) that emerged during the event.

Briefing This is a simulation in which personal consultants in the Republic of Alpha meet clients who seek experiences beyond beyond. In Alpha, the phrase 'beyond beyond' (or sometimes 'beyond the beyond') does not refer to life after death but to those parts of this life which are beyond normal experiences. It is not defined any more precisely than that. The phrase, as used by people in Alpha, indicates a degree of mystery.

There are two roles—consultants and clients—and the clients try to meet as many consultants as possible.

Consultants (probably in pairs or trios) invent the name of their consultancy and write an advertisement for the Personal Column in *Alpha News*—a limit of 20 words, including the name of the consultancy. Avoid comparisons or claims—'We are the best', 'Our service is used by top people'. Just describe some of your services and/or state your aims. Fill in the name of the consultancy on the Standard Contract forms and hand these to the clients for signing later, should they decide to accept your services.

Clients individually write in their 'My Diary Notes' a sentence or two probably beginning, 'I wish to seek beyond beyond because ...'. Clients can later show the Diary to consultants or keep it private. Clients then move from consultant to consultant and collect a Standard Contract from each consultancy. At the end of the event, and not before, clients could, if they so wish, sign one (or perhaps two) of these Contracts.

Behaviour During the consultations do not try to search for 'beyond beyond', but explore the services offered by the consultants. These could include access to books, one-to-one meetings, group meetings and so on. Do not attempt to negotiate about money or fees. All consultants charge the same fees and all clients can afford to sign up with one (or two) consultants.

Consultants Do not imitate the sort of behaviour you think appropriate to such a consultant. Be yourself, be responsible, be serious. Try to help in a creative and understanding way. Do not try to probe into personal (hypothetical) histories—concentrate on the facilities you offer for the quest.

Clients Do not imitate the sort of behaviour you think appropriate to a client seeking 'beyond beyond'. Do not play-act—keep your own personality. Whatever your own personal views about 'beyond beyond', try to be plausible in giving reasons for your quest. If you wish, you could create a hypothetical background—age, gender, race, personal history—but this might be distracting and may not be relevant. If in doubt, simply express a willingness to venture beyond the world of established facts and ask what services the consultants offer.

Alpha News Advertisement Department

Personal Column: the advertisement must not be longer than 20 words, including the name of the advertiser.

Write in capital letters.

Standard Consultancy Agreement

Name of consultancy: ....

I agree to accept the services of this consultancy on the basis of the standard fees.

Signed (client) ....

My Diary Notes

5 Conference planning

Description — A simulation about planning the timetable and contents of a conference.

Objectives — To enhance the skills of creativity, communication, planning, presentation, teamwork and time management. The simulation contains a hidden agenda—the information which is not revealed unless requested.

Time and numbers — With small numbers, the event might last for an hour. With larger numbers, more time will be needed in the debriefing for explanations and comparisons and the event could take up to two hours. The minimum number is probably six. There is no maximum number.

Resources
- Briefing sheet—one copy for each participant.
- Consultancy Test Instructions—one copy for each team.
- Three pieces of Additional Information—one each for each team (only if they request it).
- Schedule—one copy for each team.
- Scrap paper.

Method
1. Hand out the Briefing sheets. Divide the participants at random into teams of between two and five, and if there are sufficient numbers choose (at random) a team representing Alpha International Conference Centre. Set a time-limit for the end of the time-scheduling and for the end of the presentations.
2. Retrieve the Briefing sheets. Hand out copies of the Consultancy Test Instructions and the Schedule—one copy of each for each team. Make scrap paper available.
3. If there is a conference management team it should be given copies of the Additional Information to be handed out; otherwise you keep these copies (see Consultancy Test Instructions) and hand them out only when specifically requested, i.e. 'Please let us have the information about equipment' and make sure that the required two-minute period of inactivity is observed.

Debriefing — Since the presentations will have revealed the plans, the debriefing could begin by teams explaining what ideas they rejected, what their problems were and how they tackled the problems. They should also explain whether they requested any of the Additional Information, and whether, in retrospect, they should have done it sooner or differently.

If there was a management team the debriefing could also cover its work. How well did it communicate? How creative was it in devising the procedures and opportunities for presentations?

Briefing

This is a simulation about planning the schedule for a conference and presenting the plan. You are applicants for the job of consultants attached to Alpha International Conference Centre.

The Centre will shortly set up Consultancy Units to advise clients on how their conferences could be organized, and there are several vacancies for the job of consultant. There are also one or two vacancies in the Promotions and Publicity Departments.

You will be given Consultancy Test Instructions and a Schedule form, plus scrap paper. It is important to keep strictly to the deadlines.

Alpha International Conference Centre

Consultancy Test Instructions

The aim of this test is to assess the creative ability used to devise a schedule for a conference and to present this plan to the other applicants and to the management team. Do not be tempted to request extra time—your ability to manage time is one of the skills we shall be assessing.

A hypothetical organization, the Beta Teachers' and Trainers' Association, has booked a conference and our consultants have been asked to produce a schedule. It must start at 9 a.m. and continue to 5 p.m. with a 30-minute break in the morning and a 30-minute break in the afternoon, plus one hour for lunch. The schedule should be flexible enough to cope with last-minute changes.

Three rooms are available: a large room which has seating capacity for all the members of the conference, a medium-sized room which could accommodate half the members and a smaller room which could accommodate one-third of the members. One video machine is allocated and can be used in any of the rooms.

The conference is entitled 'Teaching Techniques for Today and Tomorrow' and must allow separate presentations (workshops, activities) on nine themes, each of which can be used by the presenters to illustrate aspects of techniques:

- Assessment—a session to sum up and assess activities.
- Drama—a drama, play-acting, role-play.
- Exercise—a group activity with participants in the role of problem solvers.
- Game—a competitive activity with a scoring mechanism.
- Icebreaker—an activity to break 'ice', allowing people to meet as many other people as possible.
- Lecture—an instructional talk (demonstration, speech) usually followed by questions.
- Seminar—a small group discussion led by an instructor/teacher/trainer.
- Simulation—a group activity with participants in functional roles.
- Video demonstration—instructional (or interactive) presentation using video.

These sessions can be long or short. Activities can take place in one room or several. They can overlap each other or be in parallel sessions.

Additional information is available from the Catering Department, the Equipment Department and from the Beta Teachers' and Trainers' Association, but to obtain this information requires the team to sacrifice time by sitting for two minutes (a full 120 seconds) without speaking, writing or communicating for each separate piece of information requested. Thus to acquire all three pieces of information a group would have to sit silently for six minutes without doing any work (including reading). Contact the management team if you wish to have one or more of the three pieces of information.

All planning must be completed by the deadline and the presentations follow immediately. We hope that all members of your team will participate in your presentation as we do have vacancies in our Promotions and Publicity Departments and are looking for creative and sensitive communicators.

Unless you are the first team to make a presentation, divide up so that you will not be tempted to continue your planning in the presentation period. You must accept that you are a privileged audience for the presentations and behave respectfully and politely.

Additional Information

Catering Department
Due to transport difficulties, no lunches will be available until 1 p.m. although tea, coffee and biscuits will be provided as required.

Equipment Department
The video equipment will not be available until 2 p.m.

Teachers' and Trainers' Association
A VIP will be visiting the conference at 3 p.m. and expects to see a demonstration of the drama technique.

Catering Department
Due to transport difficulties, no lunches will be available until 1 p.m. although tea, coffee and biscuits will be provided as required.

Equipment Department
The video equipment will not be available until 2 p.m.

Teachers' and Trainers' Association
A VIP will be visiting the conference at 3 p.m. and expects to see a demonstration of the drama technique.

Catering Department
Due to transport difficulties, no lunches will be available until 1 p.m. although tea, coffee and biscuits will be provided as required.

Equipment Department
The video equipment will not be available until 2 p.m.

Teachers' and Trainers' Association
A VIP will be visiting the conference at 3 p.m. and expects to see a demonstration of the drama technique.

Schedule

Starting time	Finishing time	Activity	Large room	Medium room	Small room

6 Cracked pot

Description A simulation dealing with the media which has an embarrassing story about the company.

Objectives To enhance the skills of creativity, communication, diplomacy, planning, teamwork and time management.

Time and numbers With small numbers, the event might last for half an hour. With larger numbers (with events run in parallel) more time will be needed in the debriefing for explanations and comparisons and the event could take about an hour. The minimum number is probably three. There is no maximum number.

Resources
- Briefing sheet—one copy for each participant.
- Faxed letter from the Managing Director—one copy for each team.
- Memo from MD's secretary—one copy for each team.
- Message from the Producer of 'Only Human'—one copy for each team.
- Scrap paper.

Method
1. Hand out the Briefing sheets—one copy for each participant. Announce a deadline for the completion of the event.
2. Retrieve all the Briefing sheets.
3. Divide the participants into teams of four. If desirable, each member of the Board could represent a different department—Finance, Sales, Design and Production. If the number will not divide into four it is possible to have teams of three by combining the role of Design and Production or enlarging a team by having an 'assistant' for one (or more) of the roles.
4. Give each team three documents: (1) a copy of the faxed letter from the Managing Director, (2) the Memo from the Managing Director's secretary and (3) the message from the Producer of 'Only Human'.
5. Make scrap paper available.

Debriefing If there are several teams, begin by finding out what they did. How did they cope? What did they decide to do and why? Did they appoint one of their number to look after press enquiries? (It seems likely that the media would want pictures and comments.) If asked for the whereabouts of the boss, should they disclose information? Did they use their imagination and create contingency plans?

The main part of the debriefing might deal with specific skills—creativity, communication, diplomacy, planning, teamwork and time management.

Briefing   In this simulation you are an executive in the company Do-It-Yourself Household Furniture in the Republic of Alpha.

The situation is explained in a faxed letter from Pat Quickly, the owner and Managing Director of the company. It concerns the Cracked Pot Award for 'awful English' which relates to instructions for the erection of a garden chair.

In addition, you will have a Memo from Pat Quickly's secretary giving the extract from the brochure.

You will also receive details of a telephone message from the Producer of 'Only Human', a television show. The call came through before you arrived at the office.

Alpha Central Hospital

To the Executives of Do-It-Yourself Household Furniture

I am faxing this to you from hospital as a matter of urgency. I am undergoing my operation this morning. Do not attempt to contact me for the next two days. I will be back in the office by the end of next week.

   Late last night on the hospital radio I heard an item of news to the effect that a society I have never heard of—The Society for Sensible English—has awarded our company its Cracked Pot Award for awful English. I gather it refers to instructions in one of our brochures about a garden chair. Find out what it is all about. Either ignore it or do something effective. It may or may not be worth pointing out to this obscure Society that all our brochures are written by experts—the people who design the furniture. I shall require a full report on my return, plus any comments or recommendations.

Pat Quickly

Do-It-Yourself Household Furniture

Inter-office Memorandum

To: Executives

From: Pat Quickly's secretary

I have received a copy of Pat's faxed letter and realize that you may require the extract from the brochure dealing with the garden chair. I understand that the designer who wrote this item left the company six months ago and apparently had been offered a position abroad. Nothing further is known. Here is the extract:

Garden Chair—instruction for the erection thereof. The Garden Chair (Model 53/C) is ideal for picnics or barbecues or any other outdoor activity in which people are likely to be seated and this particular model can take two (or three thin) persons and the assembly erection should begin by placing the device upside down on the ground or patio (possibly on a groundsheet if the ground is damp in order to avoid damage to the seat) and the three legs should then be firmly grasped or held and pulled into a vertical or upright position and secured by metal securing devices (metal clamps) so that they are held rigid whereupon the seat or legs (or both) can be elevated and inverted (lifted and turned upside down, now right way up) so that the seat is uppermost and the three legs planted firmly on the surface which should not be so soft or damp that the legs sink in, nor placed on stony or uneven ground where the erection might collapse, nor on sloping ground which could affect the general stability of the device.

Telephone message

Timed 09.14

Danny, producer of 'Only Human' on Alpha Television, has telephoned to invite a representative of the company to attend a televised award presentation at prime time this evening. He said that because a 'cracked pot' does not exist, the TV Props Department are constructing a large vessel, suitably cracked. The pot will be presented by the President of The Society for Sensible English. Danny said the matter was urgent as arrangements have to be made. He added that if no one is able to represent the company the pot will be presented to 'one of our girls'. Please contact Danny of 'Only Human' as soon as possible.

7 Creations

Description   A simulation about designing fashions involving the theme of the theatre.

Objectives   To enhance the skills of creativity, artistry, communication, diplomacy, planning, presentation, teamwork and time management.

Time and numbers   With small numbers, the event might last for an hour. With larger numbers, more time will be needed in the debriefing for explanations and comparisons and the event could take about two hours. The minimum number is probably six. There is no maximum number.

Resources
- Briefing sheet—one copy for each participant.
- Design and Presentation Test—one copy for each participant.
- Scrap paper, including some large sheets, plus coloured pens.

Method
1. Hand out the Briefing sheets—one to each participant. Fix a deadline for the start and end of the presentations. Discuss the facilities.
2. Retrieve the Briefing sheets.
3. Divide the participants into teams of between two and five, and if there are sufficient numbers have a team representing management which could observe what happens and also decide on the order of presentations. Possibly the management team could address the applicants at the end of the presentations.
4. Hand out the Design and Presentation Test sheet—one to each participant—and make available the scrap paper, large paper and coloured pens.

Debriefing   Since the presentations will be seen by everyone, the debriefing could start with teams revealing what ideas they rejected and how they worked together on both the designs and the presentations.

    The debriefing will then probably focus on the skills involved, including the skills of any management team.

Briefing

This is a simulation about applicants for the job of trainee designers at Alphahouse Fashions. As part of the selection procedure, teams of applicants are given the task of designing fashions based on the theme of the theatre. The procedure is explained in the Memo, and sufficient materials are provided for the designs. In addition, the teams have to present their designs, explaining and describing their ideas.

Alphahouse Fashions
Design and Presentation Test

This test is to give opportunities for design and presentation. Both are equally important because we have vacancies not only for trainee designers but also in the Publicity and Promotions Departments.

We are looking for creativity, artistry, and skills in communication, diplomacy, planning, teamwork and time management.

Your task is to work as a team to produce fashion designs based on the theme of the theatre. This could be any aspect of the theatre and could be for men, women or both. If you cannot think of an idea, use the theme of the opera 'Carmen' and design Spanish costumes.

Our advice is that you do not spend all your time and energies on designing and omit to discuss the method of presentation. Ideally, each member of your team should have a part in the presentation. Last year one team failed to discuss presentation and tried to do it during the presentation of another team. We had to disqualify the whole team, which was a pity since some of them showed creativity and flair. So make sure that you do not talk or write during other teams' presentations.

8 Cup and clip

Description A simulation dealing with job stress as represented by a cup and a paper-clip.

Objectives To enhance the skills of creativity, communication, counselling, diplomacy and time management. It can be used as an icebreaker.

Time and numbers With small numbers the event might last for half an hour and with larger numbers the event may last for an hour or so. The minimum number is probably six. There is no maximum number.

Resources
- Briefing sheet—one copy for each participant.
- Guide to the Introductory Activity—one copy for each participant.
- A cup with a paper-clip—one for each pair.
- Signalling device (bell, whistle, buzzer).

Method
1 Hand out the Briefing sheets, one for each participant. Set a time-limit for the meetings. This depends largely on the time available and the number of participants, but it is desirable to give everyone an opportunity to meet everyone else while allowing sufficient time for each meeting. About two minutes per meeting is the minimum. Arrange for some timing signal—bell, whistle, buzzer, banging a desk—for couples to separate and find new partners. If there are large numbers, it may be a good idea to have a team representing the Alpha Health and Caring Council who would supervise the meetings and movements.
2 Retrieve all the Briefing sheets and hand out the Guide to the Introductory Activity.
3 Allow the participants several minutes to read this and discuss any points that might arise—but do not go so far as to discuss the substance (as distinct from the mechanics) of the event.
4 If there is no management team, watch for the situation in which all the clients have met all the helpers and a change of roles is required for meetings to continue. If there is a management team, they should, if necessary, supervise this situation.

5 At the end of the activity the management team might wish to say a few words. There could be a discussion which would be similar to a debriefing, but in role.

Debriefing

Begin the debriefing with each person, including any management team, giving a brief description of their experiences in the event. The subsequent discussion could cover the skills—creativity, communication, counselling, diplomacy and time management. If the main purpose was to use the event as an icebreaker, the discussion could focus on this aspect.

Briefing

In this simulation you are applicants for jobs with the Alpha Health and Caring Council. The situation is explained in the Guide to the Introductory Activity.

Do not play-act, mimic or give a dramatic performance of a distressed person or adopt a 'funny' voice or dramatic mannerisms as a helper. The client should objectively describe the stress problems. Remember, your role is a person seriously applying for a job—a comic performance will not impress the assessors favourably.

Alpha Health and Caring Council

Guide to the Introductory Activity

Welcome to our one-day Assessment Procedure. Basically, we are looking for helpers (counsellors, advisers, receptionists)—people who will be in personal contact with clients and patients.

Our Introductory Activity is an icebreaker—designed for applicants to get to know each other on a person-to-person basis in the context of caring.

One member of each pair must have the role of client and hold a cup and a paper-clip. This participant must use the cup and clip as a metaphor of job stress. If you cannot think of a metaphor, then say 'I feel like the clip in this cup, I cannot seem to relate properly, I feel trapped and anxious at work'. You can take the clip out of the cup, but do not bend the clip or damage the cup. The helper can ask questions or offer advice, but the main task is to listen sympathetically.

Meetings must end immediately on the time signal, even if you are in mid-sentence. At the end of the meeting the client gives the cup and clip to the helper and the two change roles for their next meeting. Your job is to meet as many other applicants as possible and avoid meeting the same person twice.

After several meetings, you may find that a person you wish to meet is in the same role as yourself, in which case try to exchange roles (giving or receiving cup and clip) with someone else.

Although the aim of the activity is to break the ice, certain skills may be involved—creativity, communication, counselling, diplomacy and time management—and we shall be on the look-out for proficiency in such skills. For example, if a pair seems unable to observe the time-limit we might draw the conclusion that their time management skills could be improved.

One warning. Do not put on dramatic performances! As both client and helper you must keep your own personalities. Sobbing and extravagant gestures are out! Clients should describe their (hypothetical) experiences and problems objectively. Helpers should be helpful and 'professional'.

9 Cutie Cat

Description A simulation in which a debt recovery company plans to use embarrassment.

Objectives To enhance the skills of creativity, communication, planning, presentation, teamwork and time management.

Time and numbers With small numbers, the event might last for half an hour. If there are several teams, more time will be needed in the debriefing for explanations and comparisons and the event could take about an hour. The minimum number is probably six. There is no maximum number.

Resources
- Briefing sheet—one copy for each participant.
- Memo—one copy for each participant.
- Worksheet—one copy for each group.
- Scrap paper.

Method
1. Hand out the Briefing sheets—one for each participant—and discuss the facilities, the time-limits and the location of the teams.
2. Retrieve all the Briefing sheets and divide the participants (at random) into teams.
3. If there are sufficient numbers, one team could represent the directors and take charge of the mechanics of the event, and perhaps lead a discussion afterwards about what action the agency might take.
3. Hand out the Memo and the Worksheet—one copy for each team—and make scrap paper available.

Debriefing It is a good idea to start with each team debriefing themselves and then taking it in turns to announce (without discussion) which ideas they recommended and which ideas they rejected. This puts everyone in the picture and the subsequent discussion can cover what actually happened. If there is a team representing the directors, show them these notes during the course of the event. The discussion can cover the skills involved. For example, under the heading of creativity, did any team suggest bringing Friendly, the mouse, into the action?

Briefing

You are executives at the Alpha Debt Recovery Agency and your job is to explore the possibilities of using Cutie Cat to embarrass debtors into paying up. The situation is explained in a memo from your Managing Director.

Cutie Cat was the name of a character in an old newspaper comic strip in the Republic of Alpha. It was popular at the time, when the character was regarded as clever, funny and attractive, but is now regarded as being over-sweet, twee and cloying. This character, sometimes accompanied by a friendly mouse called Friendly, had adventures in which Cutie Cat tried to help other characters, sometimes successfully and sometimes making a mess of things. Although the cartoon has not been seen for many years it is still remembered, and there is a well-known saying in Alpha 'Don't be a Cutie Cat', meaning something along the lines of 'Don't be twee, precocious, cloying, self-satisfied and prissy'.

Alpha Debt Recovery Agency

MEMO

From: Managing Director

To: Executives

As part of our softly softly approach I want you to explore the possibility of obtaining repayment from debtors by embarrassing them with a person dressed up as Cutie Cat. These debtors are not the 'can't pays' who are suffering hardship and with whom we negotiate. They are the 'have money but won't pay' type. Polite letters are ineffective, legal action is difficult and expensive, and intimidation is out.

Divide into teams, each team coming up with ideas—the location of Cutie Cat's appearance and the action taken by Cutie Cat. The action must, of course, be legal and give rise to humour, not bullying. Incidentally, our lawyers have told us that the copyright on the character has long since expired. I enclose a Worksheet which you might find handy to list your ideas—the locations of the meetings, the action scenario, plus any comments you feel are relevant.

After meeting in teams, have a joint session and:

(a) put forward a coherent plan; and
(b) indicate which team (or person) could be responsible for which aspect.

Worksheet

Location	Action	Comments
Example 1		
Example 2		
Example 3		

10 Demotivate

Description A simulation in which consultants create plans to demotivate staff.

Objectives To enhance the skills of creativity, communication, diplomacy, planning, teamwork and time management.

Time and numbers With small numbers, the event might last for half an hour. If there are several teams, more time will be needed in the debriefing for explanations and comparisons and the event could take about an hour. The minimum number is probably six. There is no maximum number.

Resources
- Briefing sheet—one copy for each participant.
- Memo—one copy for each team.
- Worksheet—one copy for each team (with some spares).
- Scrap paper.

Method
1. Hand out the Briefing sheets—one to each participant. Set a deadline for the start of the joint discussion.
2. Retrieve all the Briefing sheets. Divide the participants at random into teams of between three and six. If there are sufficient numbers, make one team (randomly chosen) the management team who will organize the mechanics of the event—particularly the joint meeting.
3. Hand out to each team a copy of the Memo and the Worksheet.
4. Make scrap paper available.

Debriefing This could begin with teams revealing the ideas they rejected during the preliminary discussions. The Worksheets could be passed round if they had not been made public earlier. Do not spend much time on the general merits of devising demotivation plans, except possibly to note that they may not be all that different from some plans for motivating the staff. The central part of the debriefing could deal with the skills shown within teams and between teams during the joint discussions. This could include the question of how the managers organized the meeting. In the absence of the Managing Director (no role) did anyone take the chair, or take minutes, or discuss an agenda?

Briefing

This is a simulation in which consultants plan to demotivate staff in the Republic of Alpha. You are executives working for Alpha Staff Consultancy Company and your job is to think of ideas and examples of how to demotivate the editorial staff of Alpha Academic and Business Press. The reason for this is explained in a Memo from your Managing Director. A Worksheet and scrap paper will be provided.

Alpha Academic and Business Press is the oldest specialist publisher in Alpha. It began more than 100 years ago as an academic publisher and now has two separate divisions—Academic and Business. The divisions operate separately, but use the same printing plant. They produce textbooks and also a small list of specialist journals. The company is now facing strong competition.

Alpha Staff Consultancy Company

MEMO

From: Managing Director

To: Managers

Strictly Confidential

After informal talks with the owner of Alpha Academic and Business Press, I have agreed to produce a plan to demotivate the editorial staff. The purpose of the plan is to find out what not to do. The staff consists of publishers, editors, designers and, by implication, authors.

Please divide into teams and answer the following hypothetical questions, giving specific hypothetical examples to illustrate any general points. The Worksheet may be of help.

1 How could the owner set about the demotivation?
2 Would it require a cover story, and if so, what?
3 What benefits could the owner personally gain from demotivating the staff?

If you are finding it difficult to answer these questions or have finished early, then approach another team and request permission to sit in with them. Finally, meet together in joint session and see if you can find a consensus.

To avoid any misunderstanding, this consultation is highly confidential and must not be disclosed to any other person.

Worksheet

Ideas	Examples
1. Demotivation	
2. Cover story	
3. Benefits for owner	

11 Deoor Advertising

Description — A simulation about advertising of a product named Deoor—or any anagram of that name.

Objectives — To enhance the skills of creativity, artistry, communication, planning, presentation, teamwork and time management.

Time and numbers — With small numbers, the event might last for half an hour. If there are several teams, more time will be needed in the debriefing for explanations and comparisons and the event could take about an hour. The minimum number is probably four. There is no maximum number.

Resources
- Briefing sheet—one copy for each participant.
- Test Instructions—one copy for each team.
- Product Advertisement sheet—one copy for each team.
- Scrap paper—including some large sheets and coloured pens.
- Presentation facilities—possibly flipchart or overhead projector.

Method
1. Hand out the Briefing sheets—one copy for each participant.
2. Set a time-limit for the beginning of the presentations. Discuss the facilities, including a presentation area, separate tables for the teams and any presentational facilities—possibly flipchart or overhead projector. Retrieve the Briefing sheets.
3. Divide the participants at random into teams of between two and five, and if there are sufficient numbers make one team (randomly chosen) the management team who will organize the mechanics of the event.
4. Hand out the Test Instructions—one to each participant. Hand out the Products Advertisement sheet—one to each team. Make available the scrap paper and some large sheets and coloured pens.
5. If there is a management team, it can perhaps say a few words to the job applicants at the end of the presentations. Since this may encroach upon the normal debriefing discussion it may be a good idea to show the management team the following debriefing notes.

Debriefing — There are about 50 possible anagrams, including deoro, deroo, doreo, edoro, erdoo, erodo, odero, odore, oerdo, oored, redoo, reodo, rodeo.

73

Probably the debriefing will concentrate on the skills the management team were looking for. This should include the skills of the management team itself—their creativity in arranging for the presentations, announcing the presentations, keeping to a time schedule, working as a team and communicating with the job applicants. For example, their Memo recommended that all members of a team should participate in the presentation. Did management conclude the event with comments from all the management team or just one person? Did they show creative flair and promotional skills, or merely say 'We will let you know'?

Briefing

You are applicants for creative jobs in Alphahouse Advertising Agency. The jobs include copywriter, promotions assistant and advertising assistant. As part of a one-day series of tests and interviews at a luxury hotel you will be asked to work as a team to devise and advertise a product with the name of Deoor, or any anagram of that word. You will receive two documents—Test Instructions and Products Advertisement Sheet, plus scrap paper.

Alphahouse Advertising Agency

Test Instructions

Thank you for applying for jobs with our Agency.

In this test you will be divided at random into teams and will have two tasks.

The first task is to devise and advertise a hypothetical product with the name Deoor, or any anagram of that word. For example, you might use the word Deroo and decide that it is a shampoo, or toothpaste, or small cuddly toy. You will have a Products Advertisement sheet. Imagine that it represents a quarter-page advertisement in a newspaper. Do not invent comic or ridiculous products.

The second task is to present your work to the other teams, plus management team. The order of presentation will be made randomly. Teams who are presenting should try to involve all members of the team. Teams who are watching presentations should split up to avoid the temptation to continue the planning and discussions in order to gain an unfair advantage. Scrap paper will be made available to help you to devise the product and present your ideas to us.

We shall be observing teams and individuals for artistry, creativity, communication, planning, presentation, teamwork and time management. For example, if a team spends so long on devising and advertising a product and neglects consideration of the presentation, then we will not be impressed by that team's planning ability or time management. Nor will we be impressed by teamwork if one or two members of a team take on the presentation, leaving the others to sit silently and nod their heads.

Alphahouse Advertising Agency

Product Advertisement

Team ....

12 Games names

Description A simulation about a developing country seeking more appropriate names for well-known games.

Objectives To enhance the skills of creativity, communication, diplomacy, negotiation, planning and teamwork. It can be used as an icebreaker.

Time and numbers With small numbers, the event might last for half an hour. If there are several teams, more time will be needed in the debriefing for explanations and comparisons and the event could take about an hour. The minimum number is probably six. There is no maximum number.

Resources
- Briefing sheet—one copy for each participant.
- Memo from Minister—one copy for each participant.
- Creating Names sheet—one copy for each participant.
- Scrap paper.

Method
1 Hand out the Briefing sheets—one copy to each participant. Discuss the time-limit and the facilities. Rearrange any furniture to allow free movement.
2 Retrieve all the Briefing sheets and hand out the Memo from the Minister—one copy for each participant.
3 Hand out the Creating Names sheet—one copy for each participant—and make scrap paper available.

Debriefing It could be useful for participants to take it in turns to mention the names they created, including those which were later discarded. The main interest will probably be in the skills shown. For example, were participants diplomatic? Did they negotiate? Did anyone say 'I will support your name if you support mine'? Were they fiercely competitive or did they cooperate?

Briefing

This is a simulation about a developing country, the Republic of Delta, seeking more appropriate names for well-known games. You are an executive at the Ministry of Leisure in Delta and you will receive a Memo from the Minister asking you individually to create names for games and sports—bridge, tennis, cricket, golf, rowing, and so on.

You will each receive a Creating Names sheet and scrap paper will be available if required.

Ministry of Leisure

MEMO

From: The Minister

To: Executives

The Cabinet has decided that Delta is losing its linguistic culture by importing too many foreign names, particularly in games and sports, and has asked me to provide a list of possible names that:

(a) are more appropriate; or
(b) sound different; or
(c) are more Deltan in origin.

On this last point, for example, few international games contain the letters J or Z or end in O or IO.

Individually devise at least one, and preferably several, new names for games and enter these on your Creating Names sheet. Then meet in pairs and write on the other executive's Creating Names sheet your comments on their names.

When you have met all the other executives, find a partner with whom you can agree on most of the names on your lists. Then seek a larger grouping until finally everyone is part of a committee which has the job of drawing up a list of the most suitable and appropriate names.

If, to begin with, you cannot think of a new name for a game, write down 'Chess' and suggest 'Checkmate', or 'Jess'.

MINISTRY OF LEISURE
Creating Names

Executive ....

Well-known game name(s) ....

New game name(s) ....

Executives	Comments

13 Guru training

Description A simulation about planning and advertising a course for training management gurus.

Objectives To enhance the skills of creativity, communication, planning, presentation and teamwork. The event can be run as an icebreaker.

Time and numbers With small numbers the event might last for an hour, but with large numbers, allow up to two hours. The minimum number is probably eight. There is no maximum number.

Resources
- Briefing sheet—one copy for each participant.
- Memo from Managing Director—one copy for each participant.
- Guru Territory sheet—one copy for each participant.
- Scrap paper.

Method
1 Hand out the Briefing sheets, one to each participant. Discuss the time-limit and the facilities, including an arrangement of furniture which allows for free movement.
2 Retrieve all the Briefing sheets. Hand out the Memo from the Managing Director and the Guru Territory sheet—one copy of each to each participant.
3 Make scrap paper available.

Debriefing Most participants will have learned other people's ideas about the training of gurus, so it might be useful to begin by considering whether the Managing Director would be pleased with the outcome—not simply the idea but also the creativity, communication skills, planning and teamwork. Another aspect is the range of the plans. Did they deal with such matters as publicity and advertising? If not, why not? Did anyone suggest that the media might be interested in such a course? Finally, if the main reason for running the event was the icebreaker format, how well did it break the ice?

Briefing

Alpha Training Systems in the Republic of Alpha is contemplating courses for the training of management gurus. You are an executive and you will receive a Memo from the Managing Director telling you what to do. In addition you will have a sheet entitled 'Guru Territory' on which to enter your ideas.

The procedure, as explained in the Memo, is that you should start as individuals, fill in an idea on your form and then obtain written comments from other participants.

It is important to meet as many other participants as possible and as privately as possible. Do not linger too long in any one meeting.

Alpha Training Systems

MEMO

From: Managing Director

To: All executives

As part of our Specialized Residential Courses we are contemplating the possibility of a course for the training of Management Gurus. You know what I mean. You have read their books. How can we train people to be like them? Naturally, we do not expect many candidates to reach the highest ranks of the profession, but some may and most others should gain personal and professional benefits as a result of the course.

Please participate in the following three-part procedure:

1. Begin individually by writing down at least one idea on the subject. If you cannot think of an idea, then join another executive and work as a pair.

2. Take your idea round to other individuals (or pairs) and ask them to write their comments on your form. Try to have a face-to-face meeting with everyone.

3. Having met every other executive (or pair of executives), join up into pairs, trios or foursomes if the ideas are mutually compatible. However, do not junk promising ideas for the sake of consensus. The aim is not to form large groups, the aim is to avoid unnecessary duplication. I would be perfectly happy if there were no merging, provided the ideas were sufficiently distinctive.

I shall be looking not only for good guru territory creativity but also for good communication skills, planning and teamwork.

Guru territory

Name ....

Idea ....

....

....

Names	Comments

14 I, Anxious

Description A simulation about the house magazine of a large company seeking assistant editors for an 'Anxious' page.

Objectives To enhance the skills of creativity, communication, counselling, teamwork and time management in a situation which might involve aspects of gender and race.

Time and numbers With small numbers, the event might last for an hour. If there are large numbers, more time will be needed in the debriefing for explanations and comparisons and the event could take up to two hours. The minimum number is six. There is no maximum number.

Resources
- Briefing sheet—one copy for each participant.
- Memo—(two pages) one copy for each participant.
- 'Anxious' form—one copy for each team (with a few spares).
- Comments form—one copy for each team (with a few spares).
- Scrap paper.

Method
1 Hand out the Briefing sheets—one copy for each participant. Discuss the facilities available. Set deadlines for completion of (a) the letter, (b) the reply, (c) the assessment and (d) the comments.
2 Retrieve all the Briefing sheets.
3 Divide the participants at random into teams of two, three or four, arranged at three separate tables in triangular formation to facilitate the passing round of the 'Anxious' form. The tables should be relatively far apart. With 12 participants, there could be three teams of four or the event could be run in parallel with two groups of three tables each. With larger numbers, run the event in parallel with two or more groups of three tables.
4 Give each participant a copy of the Memo. Give each team a copy of the 'Anxious' form and the Comments form. Make scrap paper available.
5 As stressed in the Memo, it is important that each team should hand their document to the next team on time, otherwise the waiting team is likely to become impatient.

Debriefing

This could start with each team debriefing itself, particularly in relation to creativity, communication, counselling, teamwork and time management. The teams could then join together and each team announce what they had written on their Comments form. The general discussion could then cover such issues as the plausibility of the letters and replies and whether they raised matters such as gender, race, age, etc. How sensitively were the issues handled? Were the replies to the letters sincere, caring, lucid and appropriate? Did the assessments note strengths as well as weaknesses, or were they simply arguments saying 'Our contribution was best'?

Did the teams work well together? Did they cooperate on managing the time factor? What ideas did they think of and then discard?

Briefing

You are applicants for the job of Assistant Editor to a new house magazine devoted to the staff issues of a large company in the Republic of Alpha—Alpha Bus and Rail Company. The magazine will have an 'Anxious' page.

What you have to do is explained in the Memo, which you will receive after being divided into one or more groups of three teams. You will receive an 'Anxious' form which must be passed (promptly on the deadline) to the next team in a clockwise direction.

Do not play-act the roles (functions). You keep your own personality, but take on new duties and responsibilities. For example, if you wrote a comic or absurd letter it would be unfair to the team which had to answer it and you would not create a favourable impression with the Appointments Department.

ALPHA BUS AND RAIL

MEMO

From: Appointments Department

To: Candidates for the position of Assistant Editor

Thank you for applying for the job of Assistant Editor on our new Staff Magazine which will have a page devoted to letters and replies to staff who are anxious about aspects of work.

The first test involves you:

(a) working as a team
(b) working to very strict deadlines

which we deem essential qualifications for the job. We also hope to see something of your creative abilities, your communication skills and how sensitive and sensible you are when trying to help people who are anxious.

The deadlines referred to are the times for passing on the 'Anxious' form to the next team in a clockwise direction. The work itself must be completed before each deadline.

(1) Write a letter from a hypothetical member of staff to the 'Anxious' page about stress, anxieties or fears at work. If you think it relevant, your letter can indicate background information such as age, gender, race, nature of the job, and so on. The letter should:

(a) relate to work, not family matters;
(b) ask for advice, not information;
(c) be about personal anxieties, not a letter of complaint about other members of staff;
(d   be brief and to the point, not rambling;
(e) be sensible, not hysterical or ridiculous.

Use scrap paper if you wish to draft the letter. Write the letter in the letter section ONLY of the 'Anxious' form and write nothing in the other sections. Sign your letter 'Anxious'. On the deadline pass it clockwise to the next team.

(Continued)

(2) Upon receiving the letter from your neighbouring team you take on the role of an Assistant Editor and write your reply in the second section, headed 'Reply'. It must contain specific advice and not simply a 'Go and see X' response. On the deadline, pass on the form clockwise to the next team.

(3) Take on the function of a member of the Personnel Department who has been asked to assess both the letter and the reply. Write your views in the 'Assessment' Section. On the deadline, pass on the form clockwise to the next team (that wrote the original letter).

(4) Use the Comments form to comment on:
    (a) your original letter;
    (b) the reply; and
    (c) the assessment.

For example, do you need to say anything more about the letter or its hypothetical author? Was the reply likely to help 'Anxious' and was the assessment fair?

Thank you for your cooperation. We may ask you questions about this activity during the final interview.

Anxious

First task: Letter to the 'Anxious' page

....
....
....
....
....
....

Second task: Reply to the letter in the 'Anxious' page

....
....
....
....
....
....

Third task: Assessment of both letter and reply

....
....
....
....
....
....

Comments

Names of team

....

....

Comments

....

....

....

....

....

....

....

....

....

....

....

....

....

....

....

....

....

15 Island development

Description A simulation about tobacco company executives planning to buy and use an island.

Objectives To enhance the skills of creativity, communication, planning, presentation, teamwork and time management.

Time and numbers With small numbers, the event might last for half an hour. If there are several teams, more time will be needed in the debriefing for explanations and comparisons and the event could take about an hour. The minimum number is probably six. There is no maximum number.

Resources
- Briefing sheet—one copy for each participant.
- Memo—one copy for each participant.
- Scrap paper and perhaps aids to presentation—flipchart, overhead projector, etc.

Method *Note:* It is possible, particularly if the participants are new to creative events, that one or two will personally object to having a hypothetical role in a hypothetical tobacco company, so it could be a good idea to mention the subject matter before running the event. If someone does object, there are several options: (a) don't run the event at all, (b) announce that the Tobacco Division was sold yesterday, or (c) ask those who are unhappy with the idea whether they would either help you as facilitator or take on the role of reporter from Alpha Television covering the event as part of a documentary about the company.

1. Hand out the Briefing sheets—one copy for each participant. Deal with the time-limits and the facilities for presentation.
2. Retrieve all the Briefing sheets.
3. Divide the participants into teams of between two and five and separate them as far as possible to reduce intrusive noise. If the numbers are sufficient, include a management team.
4. Hand out the Memo—one copy for each participant. Make scrap paper available. If there is a management team, ask them to organize the

facilities, including the order of presentation. Emphasize the requirement that teams keep to the deadlines.

Debriefing

As everyone will have seen the presentations, it could be useful for each team, including any management team, to give an account of their rejected ideas, mentioning the problems they faced and how they dealt with them. The debriefing will probably concentrate on the skills involved, the creativity, communication, planning, presentation, teamwork and time management. However, a key issue is the problem of publicizing (explaining, justifying, ignoring) a product which has acquired a bad image. This aspect may be a focus of discussion, depending on how the participants feel about this issue.

Island development

Briefing You are an executive in Alpha Tobacco Company. The company has existed for many years and, as the climate in Alpha is suitable, it grows most of the tobacco it uses in its manufacture of cigarettes, cigars and pipe tobacco. Most of its sales are overseas. During the past 50 years the company has expanded to include agriculture and the manufacture of agricultural implements. It consists of three divisions: Tobacco, Agriculture (mainly fruit and vegetables) and Agricultural Machinery.

You will receive a Memo from the Board of Directors explaining the situation.

Alpha Tobacco Company

MEMO

From: Board of Directors

To: Executives

We have the option of purchasing a small island about half an hour by boat from the mainland. The island has long been uninhabited. It has no basic facilities. The island is rather barren, although it does have a hill with trees and several freshwater springs. There is not much wildlife, although it is used by some migrating birds a couple of times each year. The climate is usually temperate and the rainfall is moderate to low. It is sheltered by the mainland from most of the storms, particularly on the lee side of the hill. A survey indicates that a small harbour and/or small airstrip could be constructed to facilitate access.

If we bought the island, how could ATC use it advantageously? We hope you can create some useful suggestions. You can assume that sufficient finances would be available, but we do require value for money.

Divide into groups. Create a plan. We will announce a deadline when all work on plans must cease so that all can concentrate on the presentations. Each team should try to involve all its members in the presentation. If we buy the island, we shall be looking for executives with flair and sensitivity who can help us publicize the venture.

As you know, the Directors are concerned with the negative image of tobacco—a relatively modern development and one which would have surprised the founders of Alpha Tobacco Company. The latest figures show that of the three divisions of the Company, Agriculture (now essentially fruit and vegetables) is the largest in value with 38 per cent, the Agricultural Machinery Division is valued at 32 per cent and Tobacco at 30 per cent.

16 Jokes Inc.

Description A simulation in which authors and publishers plan to produce humorous books.

Objectives To enhance the skills of creativity, artistry, communication, diplomacy, planning, teamwork and time management.

Time and numbers With small numbers the event might last for an hour and with larger numbers allow up to two hours. The minimum number is probably six. There is no maximum number.

Resources
- Briefing sheet—one copy for each participant.
- Name cards for four publishers.
- Scrap paper.

Method
1. Hand out the Briefing sheets—one to each participant. Discuss the procedures and facilities.
2. Retrieve the Briefing sheets and divide the participants into two professions—publishers and authors. This could be done at random, or by giving the role of authors to those who know the most funny stories.
3. Depending on ability and inclination, the participants could decide whether to work in trios, pairs or as individuals. Preferably no more than two authors should cooperate on a work and no more than three participants should represent any one publisher. Up to four publishers are envisaged, but this could be cut to three or even two with very small numbers. With large numbers there could either be one or two extra publishing companies (creating a suitable name for their company) or the event could be run in parallel with two separate groups of publishers and authors.
4. Announce the first deadline for the completion of proposals and strategies. Also give a time-limit for each meeting—all meetings should end simultaneously as dissatisfaction can set in if some authors and publishers have to sit around with nothing to do. As mentioned in the Briefing sheet, participants can create their own breaks for contemplation by finishing a meeting a minute or two early.

Debriefing   It is a good idea to start by revealing the facts—the proposals of the authors and the views of the publishers. Ask the authors and publishers to give the facts, including any personal feelings, without discussion. Probably the main part of the debriefing would be to examine the skills—creativity, artistry, communication, diplomacy, planning, teamwork and time management.

Briefing

In this simulation you are either a publisher of humorous books or you are an author who writes humorous works and seeks a publisher. All authors should visit all publishers and discuss their proposals.

The action takes place in the Republic of Alpha where there is a great demand for humorous books.

Before the meetings start, authors should draw up a proposal and publishers should outline the areas in which they are particularly interested. There will be a time-limit for drawing up the idea, but since the meetings are exploratory it is not essential to complete all the details before the meetings begin. Scrap paper is available for notes, but no written proposals or suggestions are required.

At the meetings discuss the proposal and perhaps explore areas of possible collaboration. No firm or formal commitment must be made regarding publication as the aim is exploration, not decision-making. However, expectations could be raised or lowered informally.

Do not discuss royalties, advances and so on. Under Alpha law publishers and authors are protected by a standard contract.

To prevent authors or publishers from sitting around waiting, all meetings must be completed by the time-limit. If you would like short breaks for contemplation, finish the meeting a minute or two before the deadline. Time management is important.

Smiles Unlimited

Humour Publishing Company

Jokes, Inc.

Laughter Enterprises

17 Kissing campaign

Description A simulation in which the glossy magazine, *Alpha Creates*, plans a campaign for courteous gestures to replace doffing (raising) the hat.

Objectives To enhance the skills of creativity, communication, diplomacy, negotiation, teamwork and time management in a situation which might involve aspects of gender and race. The event can be used as an icebreaker.

Time and numbers With small numbers, the event might last for half an hour. If there are several teams, more time will be needed in the debriefing for explanations and comparisons and the event could take about an hour. The minimum number is probably eight. There is no maximum number.

Resources
- Briefing sheet—one copy for each participant.
- Memo—one copy for each participant.
- Manners form—one copy for each participant.
- Some device (whistle, buzzer, bell) for signalling the time-limits for meetings.

Method
1 Hand out the Briefing sheet—one copy to each participant—and discuss the facilities and time-limits—probably about 10 minutes for creating the original idea. Allow sufficient time during the action for everyone to meet everyone else.
2 Retrieve the Briefing sheets. Hand out the Memo and the Manners form—one copy of each to each participant. Arrange a signal (buzzer, bell, whistle) to mark the time-limit for each meeting.

Debriefing Since everyone will be familiar with other people's ideas for new gestures, the subsequent discussion need not centre on the viability of any gesture replacing doffing the hat, but on the proposals for a feature article or campaign or competition. What skills were employed? How well did the participants communicate and work together? Were issues of gender and race considered? Finally, if the event was run as an icebreaker, how well did it work?

Briefing *Alpha Creates* is the leading glossy magazine in the Republic of Alpha. It covers mainly clothing and fashion, but also architecture, interior decorating and social manners. You are executives, designers and editorial staff requested to create courteous gestures to replace doffing (raising) the hat. The situation is explained in a Memo from the Managing Director.

Alpha Creates

Memo

From: Managing Director

To: Executives, Designers and Editorial Staff

I want *Alpha Creates* to produce a feature article, and possibly a campaign and/or competition related to a replacement for doffing the hat.

Alas, few men now wear hats and fewer still doff them. Even raising the hat slightly is often half-hearted and self-conscious. As my wife has pointed out, doffing was essentially a male gesture. Ideally, a replacement gesture should be available to both sexes. Doffing, over the ages, could indicate many moods, intentions and courtesies. It could be deferential, perfunctory, over-polite, formal, hesitant, bold, seductive, simple or elaborate.

Let us see what alternative gestures you can come up with. Start individually and enter an idea on your Manners form. Do not invent some farcical or absurd idea—this is a serious matter and I want you to treat it seriously. It does not matter if the idea is unusual, providing it is plausible and can be used as a gesture of courtesy and respect—qualities which are often ignored in today's over-rushed and over-casual society. If you cannot think of an idea, then write 'Kissing the cheek'.

After devising an idea, meet in pairs for a few minutes, exchange ideas, and write your comments on the other person's idea on their Manners form. A signal will sound for the end of each meeting, so get down to business. You can, at any stage, modify and replace your original idea. Simply write the new or modified idea into the Idea section.

At the end of the period of meeting in pairs, form into larger groups and discuss the possibilities for:

(a)   a feature article;
(b)   a campaign; and
(c)   a competition,

or any combination of the three. Any positive plans might include suggestions for advertising and promoting the project. You can, of course, reject the whole concept.

I look forward to seeing your ideas.

Manners

Name ....

Idea ....

....

....

Names	Comments

18 Legislate

Description A simulation in which Members of Parliament try to put their election language into legislative language.

Objectives To enhance the skills of creativity, communication, diplomacy, negotiation, planning, presentation, teamwork and time management.

Time and numbers With small numbers the event might last for up to an hour and with larger numbers more than an hour should be allowed. The minimum number is probably eight. There is no maximum number.

Resources
- Briefing sheet—one copy for each participant.
- Legislation Training Day—one copy for each participant.
- Scrap paper.

Method
1. Hand out the Briefing sheets—one for each participant. Discuss the facilities and set a deadline for each of the three stages: initiation, committee and presentation.
2. Retrieve the Briefing sheets.
3. Hand out the Legislation Training Day document—one to each participant.
4. Divide the participants at random into groups of two or three. With eight or more participants, choose one or two people (at random) to be the Organizing Committee.
5. Hand out scrap paper.

Debriefing Everyone will know what legislation each group has proposed, so it could be interesting if groups took it in turns to outline their problems, explain how they tackled them and state what ideas were rejected and why. The subsequent discussion would probably cover the skills used in creating ideas and turning them into law.

Briefing

In this simulation the Environment Party of the Republic of Alpha is running a one-day course for its new Members of Parliament to help them understand the transition from the language of the election to the language of law. The situation is outlined in the Legislation Training Day document.

You can assume that the laws in Alpha are virtually identical to the laws that govern you.

Environment Party

Legislation Training Day

As new Members you will, of course, be receiving lots of advice from colleagues and members of the other Parties. However, the purpose of this one-day course is not to give you advice or information but to give you hands-on experience of transferring noble aims into sensible law. This activity has four stages.

1 Divide into small groups and create an idea for a change in the law—for example, 'Noisy fireworks should be banned'. The word, 'should' is the language of ethics—this should be done, that should be done—but it is not the language of law. To make it into law it must say something like 'It is illegal to manufacture or sell noisy fireworks' and probably define what a noisy firework is and what penalties might be imposed for those breaking the law. If you cannot think of an idea, then use the above example—try to outlaw noisy fireworks. Your measure can be unusual, but it should have a degree of plausibility and not be comic or absurd. Finally, think of a title for your measure.

2 Join with another group to act as a Legislative Committee to sharpen the language for the two measures. Do not debate whether ideas are good or bad, but concentrate on the legal language. Is it clear? Does it go too far? For example, the 'Drug Abuse Bill' might say, 'It is an offence to buy and sell drugs', but this would not only shut down most hospitals but would also cover tobacco, alcohol and even headache pills.

3 Having sharpened the legal language, each member of the original group must now take part in a short presentation as though introducing the measure in the House. It is enough to give the title of the Bill and to summarize the main provisions—but each member of the team that created the original idea should speak, if only a few words. Argument in favour of the measure is not required and is irrelevant. You are all good at arguing—the purpose of this session is to get the language right.

4 After the brief presentations there can be a general discussion and the Organizing Committee will probably say a few words.

19 Lesser offspring

Description A simulation in which consultants are visited by the sons and daughters of famous parents.

Objectives To enhance the skills of creativity, communication, counselling, diplomacy and planning.

Time and numbers With small numbers, the event might last for an hour. If there are large numbers, more time will be needed in the debriefing for explanations and comparisons and the event could take up to two hours. The minimum number is probably eight. There is no maximum number.

Resources
- Briefing sheet—one copy for each participant.
- Client profile form—one copy for each offspring.
- Advertisement form—one copy for each consultancy.
- Signalling device (bell, buzzer, whistle, banging the table).
- Scrap paper.

Method
1 Hand out the Briefing sheets—one copy for each participant.
2 Divide the participants, preferably at random, so that there is roughly the same number of offspring as there are consultancy agencies. If one or two participants may need help they could be placed on the staff of a consultancy rather than have the role of an individual client. Or two participants could share the role of one client (both being the same hypothetical offspring) and could help each other.
3 Retrieve all the Briefing sheets.
4 Set an overall time-limit for the action. Set a time-limit for each consultation—at least three minutes—as without a time-limit some participants may be sitting around and becoming impatient. Explain that you will give a signal for meetings to break up.
5 Arrange the furniture to ensure that each meeting is as private as possible. Discuss how the advertisements will be publicized—perhaps placed on a board.
6 Hand out the Advertisement form—one copy to each agency.
7 Hand out the Client profile form—one copy for each offspring.

8 Hand out scrap paper. During the action signal the times for clients to move to other consultancies.

Debriefing Since participants will not know what went on during other consultancies it could be a good idea to start with everyone taking it in turns to give a brief but factual (and non-argumentative) account of what occurred. The subsequent discussion will probably cover areas of skills, but might also venture into questions of the social problems facing offspring, particularly lesser offspring.

Briefing   There are two roles: the lesser offspring of a famous parent (or even of two famous parents); and agencies which have just been set up to advise, counsel and help such offspring. All the offspring are relatively wealthy and in good health.

The first task of the agency is to produce an advertisement offering services to lesser offspring. The advertisement, of not more than 20 words, is to be inserted in the glossy journal *Top People's Topics*. An Advertisement form will be provided.

The first job of the offspring is to determine their own age and sex. The age should be between about 15 and 30 years. Next they must outline the problem in relation to the parent, who must not be a real person. Indicate the area in which the parent is famous. Each offspring fills in a Client profile form which can be shown to the agencies.

Meetings between agencies and offspring then take place. Each meeting should be relatively brief and clients should seek to visit as many agencies as possible. Clients need make no decisions about which agency (or agencies) they intend to employ—the meetings are exploratory.

Top People's Topics

Advertisement Form

Write in capital letters. Use no more than 20 words, including the name of the advertiser.

Client Profile

Name ....

Background information (age, etc.) ....

....

....

....

....

Parent(s) ....

....

Problem ....

....

....

....

....

....

....

....

....

....

....

....

20 Lost Dreamers

Description
: A simulation in which explorers visit a long-lost Dreamers' tribe.

Objectives
: To enhance the skills of creativity, communications, diplomacy, planning, presentation and teamwork in a situation involving aspects of race. There is a hidden agenda—the Dreamers and the explorers have different aims.

Time and numbers
: With small numbers the event might last for an hour and with larger numbers allow up to two hours. The minimum number is probably eight. There is no maximum number.

Resources
:
- Briefing sheet—one copy for each participant.
- Dream Circle—one for each Dreamer.
- Alpha Society of Anthropology document—one for each explorer.
- Two rooms are desirable.

Method
:
1. Hand out the Briefing sheets. Discuss the scenario—that the two cultures meet separately (and privately) and have time to discuss their situation and prepare for the joint meeting(s) and then meet again separately to discuss their experiences. Discuss facilities. For example, the main room should be the homeland of the Dreamers, since the explorers are the visitors. Consider whether the Dreamers should have any (real) refreshments to offer. Set deadlines for (a) the arrival of the explorers, (b) the departure of the explorers and (c) the final separate discussion period on what happened and why.
2. Retrieve the Briefing sheets.
3. Divide the participants into two groups of roughly equal size. Separate them (if only one room is available it might be possible for the explorers to use a corridor, canteen or some other place where they might meet in reasonable privacy).
4. Hand the Alpha Society of Anthropology document to the explorers and the Dream Circle to the Dreamers. Make sure that all non-culture clutter is removed (homework, magazines, briefcases). Note that the explorers will arrive without even pencil and paper.
5. Before the explorers arrive, retrieve all copies of the Dream Circle and the Anthropology Society document.

Debriefing

The final and separate meetings will have prepared the ground for the debriefing, which could start with you handing out each group's document to the other group.

This could be followed by participants taking it in turns to explain (factually and without arguing) what the other group did not know. Once these facts are revealed, the discussion can proceed in appropriate directions—a discussion of the skills involved, a comparison with real-world features of different cultures with different philosophies of life, and so forth.

Briefing   You are either a member of the lost tribe of Dreamers or you are a member of an expedition of explorers from the Alpha Society of Anthropology. The facts, known to both cultures, are that a member of the Society discovered the lost tribe and spoke with one of its members. Both agreed that some members of the Society would come in peace and be welcomed with respect.

The event is in three stages. You meet separately and practise your culture, each culture having a document which outlines its philosophy. The second stage is the visit. The third stage takes place after the visit, when both cultures meet separately to discuss and evaluate their experiences.

When you receive your culture document in the first stage, practise your culture. In pairs, or in larger groups, take on the roles of the visitors or the visited and feel your way into your role. It is important not to play-act. Accept your role within your culture, accept its philosophy and accept the peaceful and respectful nature of the visit.

Hand your culture document back to the facilitator before the visit takes place.

DREAM CIRCLE

Do not ask 'What is the Dream?', for that is a question. A question is the snake that destroys the Truth and Beauty and Wisdom of the Dream. No search can find the Dream. Search destroys the Dream, questions rebuke the Dream.

The Dream comes from within.

The Dream is without question and without answer.

The Dream is a circle, an embrace nurturing Beauty and Truth.

The Dream is sharing, the Dream is caring.

All talk by Dreamers is in proverbs, metaphors and analogies. The chicken is doubt, the owl is wisdom and the eagle is powerful but is not a Dreamer. If a Dreamer wants to know, 'Is today the best time to reap the harvest?', the straight line will be avoided. The Dreamer might say, 'The chicken looks at the harvest'. The reply might be, 'The owl is not a beaver', meaning 'Now is not the best time for reaping'.

Turning the shoulder is a sign that questions must be turned and made into circles. Words must circle towards Truth and Beauty, not fly straight. If a Dreamer asks a question, the other Dreamer must turn the shoulder and smile.

If a stranger, a non-Dreamer, asks a question, a Dreamer should also smile and also turn the shoulder. But to the non-Dreamer's question there is a reply which can be given, 'The eagle sees the straight line, but the owl sees the circle'.

Remember, my children, the Dream is in the Circle and the Circle is in the Dream.

Alpha Society of Anthropology

To: Members of the expedition

Our last meeting was for members who wished to take part in an expedition and who were willing to take an oath of secrecy. This you did. Thank you for agreeing to come here today to practise what should be done when meeting Dreamers.

The Motives: It is essential that we do not shatter their Dream, whatever it may be. No one must take any recording devices—no cameras, no tape recorders and not even a notebook. We must not contaminate their culture. We must be friendly and cautious. If anything goes wrong, we must retreat and discuss what happened and why.

The Preparations: The present meeting is for you to practise what you will do when you meet the Dreamers. Discuss what questions you will ask, what you will say, what you will do, whether you will meet them as a group or mingle individually. Actually do it—pretend that one or more of you are Dreamers and the others can try out various approaches. Experiment, mingle, separate, intermingle. Then we can meet as a committee to agree on an approach.

21 Management poetry

Description
: A simulation about a magazine running a competition for poems about management.

Objectives
: To enhance the skills of creativity, artistry, communication, planning, presentation, teamwork and time management.

Time and numbers
: With small numbers the event might last for an hour and, with larger numbers, the event can last up to two hours. The minimum number is probably eight. There is no maximum number.

Resources
: - Briefing sheet—one copy for each participant.
  - Top Desk Competition document—one copy for each participant.
  - The use of a second room could be useful.
  - Scrap paper.

  Note: Although real video cameras and/or microphones would add to the authenticity, the participants should be experienced in their use, otherwise there could be unauthentic embarrassment, muddle and delay.

Method
: 1. Hand out the Briefing sheets—one copy for each participant. Discuss the timing of the event and to what extent the judges and the television presenters will arrange or rearrange the furniture and announce deadlines, and so on. Retrieve all the Briefing sheets.
  2. Divide the participants at random into three groups: (a) authors, (b) judges and (c) television presenters. With eight participants, there could be five authors, two judges and one television presenter. With 16 participants, there could be 10 authors, three judges and three television presenters, or the event could be run with two separate groups of eight.
  3. Hand out the Top Desk Competition document—one to each participant.
  4. Make sure that the conditions (arrangement of furniture, use of second room, etc.) allow privacy and freedom from noisy intrusions. As the location is the best hotel in town, any extra comforts or facilities (clipboards, coffee and biscuits, carafe of water, potted plants) could enhance the authenticity.
  5. Hand out scrap paper.

Debriefing

Although everyone will have seen and heard the poems and the presentation of the awards, it could be useful to start with participants taking it in turns to explain their problems and how they tackled them. The subsequent discussion should not concentrate on whether the judges did a good job in their selection but rather on the skills used by participants—artistic, media, communication, presentation, and so on.

The discussion could also look at real-life comparisons. For example, did the judges award the third prize first and the first prize last?

Briefing In the Republic of Alpha, *Top Desk* is a management magazine aimed at senior executives. Its readership is nationwide and, in order to publicize the magazine, it has been decided to hold a competition for the Best Poem on Management, and to present a prize to the winners at a ceremony at the best hotel in town.

You are either an executive who has written a poem and been selected for the shortlist, or one of a panel of judges, or a member of the television team which is covering the event live on Alpha TV2 Channel.

If you are an author (poet) you could, if you wish, seek to work in collaboration with another poet, but it is preferable to try on your own.

A letter from *Top Desk* addressed to the authors on the shortlist (but available to judges and television presenters) outlines the proceedings.

TOP DESK

Competition

Thank you very much for attending the final selection and prize-giving for Best Poem on Management and we have much pleasure in welcoming you to the final selection and prize-giving ceremony.

You were selected because of the excellence of your first poem, and all of you will receive a prize—a cheque and one year's free subscription to *Top Desk*.

However, we wish to award three further prizes—first, second and third—for a new poem about management.

The judges will explain the procedure—each poet is expected to read his or her entry—and no work on the poem is allowed after the start of the poetry reading.

There are four conditions:

1. The poem must be about management—in any form or aspect.
2. It must be at least four lines in length but not more than 20 lines altogether.
3. The action in the poem must have one (and only one) of the following locations: boardroom, office, factory, restaurant, golf course.
4. Whatever the merit of the poem it must be seriously intended—this is a competition for poetry, not comic verse.

The structure of the poem is up to you. It can rhyme, or it can be in blank verse.

You do not have to write a poem praising management. We are looking for poetry, not praise.

Thank you again for your cooperation. We hope you enjoy the experience and look forward to hearing your work.

22 Maze metaphor

Description — A simulation in which the counselling service of a large company devises a scheme involving a maze.

Objectives — To enhance the skills of creativity, artistry, communication, counselling, planning, presentation, teamwork and time management.

Time and numbers — With small numbers, the event might last for half an hour. If there are several teams, more time will be needed in the debriefing for explanation, comparisons and comments and the event could take about an hour. The minimum number is probably four. There is no maximum number.

Resources
- Briefing sheet—one copy for each participant.
- Memo—one copy for each team.
- Scrap paper and perhaps aids to presentation—flipchart, overhead projector, etc.

Method
1 Hand out the Briefing sheets—one copy for each participant. Deal with the time-limits and the facilities for presentation.
2 Retrieve all the Briefing sheets.
3 Divide the participants into teams of between two and five and separate them as far as possible to reduce intrusive noise. If the numbers are sufficient, include a team representing the directors.
4 Hand out the Memo—one copy for each team. Make scrap paper available, plus any equipment for the presentations. If there is a management team, ask them to organize the facilities, including the order of presentation. Emphasize the requirement that teams keep to the deadlines.
5 Make sure that the arrangement of furniture for the presentations is appropriate. If participants simply remain in their groups and turn their chairs, the atmosphere is lacking in respect and professionalism and the simulation is lacking in credibility.

Debriefing — As everyone will have seen the presentations, it could be useful for each team (including directors) to give an account of their rejected ideas, mentioning the problems they faced and how they dealt with them. The debriefing will probably concentrate on the skills involved—the creativity, teamwork, planning, presentation, communication and time management. Did any team's maze take account of the company's business—engineering and construction? It could be useful to compare the ideas with those of the real world—the use of a maze metaphor (a) to represent uncertainty, doubts and perhaps fears and/or (b) to indicate a clarification of a problem or a path to its solution.

Briefing This is a simulation in which the Counselling Department of a large company has the job of devising schemes involving the metaphor of a maze.

You are staff working in the Counselling Department and you will be divided into teams which will present their ideas to management.

The procedures are set out in a company Memo.

Alpha Engineering and Construction Company

Inter-office Memorandum

From: Directors, Counselling Department

To: Staff of Counselling Department

Our department has been asked to produce plans to deal with the problem of absenteeism and work-related stress within the company. We have been specifically asked to use the idea of a maze. If the ideas within these plans should have a wider application, they might be used to promote the image of the company.

Divide into teams and come up with some ideas. Here are some applications of the idea which you might wish to consider, but we do not wish to put ideas into your heads. We hope you will put ideas into our heads. Have no hesitation in choosing your own approach:

1 An activity which uses a maze.
2 A leaflet or poster using a maze.
3 A video/computer simulation.

Try out your basic ideas. Counsel someone and see if it works. Then make a presentation of your idea to the Directors, with each member of your team taking part.

23 Praise, blame

Description — A simulation about a meeting of management, staff and customers of a travel agency.

Objectives — To enhance the skills of creativity, communication, diplomacy, teamwork and time management. The event could be run as an icebreaker.

Time and numbers — With small numbers the event might last for half an hour and with larger numbers allow up to an hour. The minimum number is probably nine. There is no maximum number.

Resources
- Briefing sheet—one copy for each participant.
- Social Event document—one copy for each participant.
- Ideas form—one copy for each participant.
- Function card—one (of three functions) for each participant.
- Signalling device (whistle, buzzer, bell).
- Refreshments might be provided.

Method
1. Arrange for the number of Function Cards to match the number of participants, with equal numbers in the three roles—management, staff and customers.
2. Hand out the Briefing sheets—one copy for each participant. Discuss the facilities, including the arrangement of the furniture, and set time-limits for the meetings. Refreshments would add to the plausibility of the event.
3. Retrieve all the Briefing sheets.
4. A good way to achieve randomness is to shuffle the Function cards, place them face down and ask participants to pick their own card.
5. Hand out the Social Event document and the Ideas form—one of each for each participant.

Debriefing — It is probably a good idea to begin with participants taking it in turns to give a brief account of their experiences, their problems and the results. The general discussion could concentrate on the skills involved—the creating of complaints/suggestions, the quality of the communication, the development of teamwork and the skill of time management.

The discussion can also cover the way things developed. For example, did management voluntarily take over duties—perhaps offering refreshments or thanking staff and customers at the end of the series of meetings? If the event was run as an icebreaker, how well did it work?

Briefing

This is a simulation about a meeting of management, staff and customers of Alpha First Travel Agency.

The travel agency has arranged a social gathering so that people involved with the agency can meet freely (in pairs) and exchange their views about travel and holidays. A Social Event document explains the situation and an Ideas form is for recording praise or blame. You will receive a Function card to identify your function (status)—customer, staff, management.

- Customers—people who have made a firm booking for a holiday with the agency this year.
- Staff—mainly counter staff; only those employees in direct contact with customers.
- Management—senior administrative staff who rarely, if ever, meet customers face-to-face.

You will receive an Ideas form for praise and blame. You do not necessarily have to praise or criticize someone else. Your original praise/blame idea could be self-criticism or self-praise. For example, customers could criticize or praise their own behaviour or the behaviour of other customers.

Although the agency document does not say so, the social evening is not intended to be a session for wage negotiations. The praise and blame should relate solely to travel and holidays.

If you have to invent 'facts', make sure that they are reasonable and plausible ('Sometimes there are not enough chairs for customers'). Any such 'fact' can be accepted or challenged. If a dispute about 'facts' arises, you could ask the facilitator to give a ruling.

Alpha First Travel Agency

Social Event

Welcome to our Special Social Event. We want you to enjoy yourselves, to talk about our holiday and travel plans, to explore ways in which the agency can help customers and our customers can help us. Please feel free to say what you think.

In the spirit of 'getting to know people' we want everyone to meet in pairs, briefly, until everyone has met everyone else. To make it easier we will signal the end of meetings—so no one will be standing around waiting for others to stop talking.

For the record, we would like you to use the Ideas form. Start by writing down an idea of your own. Then meet people (in pairs only) and write comments on their forms about their ideas. If the other person agrees with your idea, then write your idea on the other person's form. Even if the person whom you meet is of the same status as yourself (customer, staff, management) you should still exchange ideas.

Alpha First Travel Agency

Ideas

Name .... Function ....

My idea ....

....

....

Name	Function	Idea or comment

Function cards

customer	staff	management
customer	staff	management
customer	staff	management
customer	staff	management

24 Pursuers, Pursued

Description A simulation in which the staff at a television company are either Pursuers or Pursued.

Objectives To enhance the skills of creativity, communication, diplomacy, negotiation, planning and teamwork.

Time and numbers With small numbers the event might last for an hour and with larger numbers allow more than an hour. The minimum number is probably eight. There is no maximum number.

Resources
- Briefing sheets—one copy for each participant.
- Professional Activity document—one copy for each participant.
- Job cards—one (of three roles) for each participant.
- Action cards—one (of two roles) for each participant, with several spare cards.

Method
1. Arrange for the number of Job cards to match the number of participants, with equal numbers in the three roles—producers, scriptwriters and actors.
2. Arrange for the number of Action cards to match the number of participants, with equal numbers in the two roles—Pursuers and Pursued—plus some spares.
3. Hand out the Briefing sheets—one copy for each participant. Discuss the facilities, including the arrangement of the furniture.
4. Retrieve all the Briefing sheets.
5. A good way to achieve randomness is to shuffle the Job cards and the Action cards separately, place them face down and ask participants to pick one of each. Keep a few extra Action cards handy so that participants can change their action category during the event.
6. Hand out the Professional Activity document—one copy for each participant.

Debriefing It is probably a good idea to begin with participants taking it in turns to give a brief account of their experiences, their problems and the results.

The general discussion could concentrate on the skills involved—creativity of projects, communication, the development of teamwork and the skill of time management. The discussion can also cover the way things developed. For example, did some people feel happier as a Pursuer or as a Pursued? Did professional agreements emerge? Did actors and scriptwriters help each other to any extent?

Briefing A simulation in which staff of the Drama Department of Alpha Television are either Pursuers or Pursued.

Everyone has one of three jobs—actor, producer, scriptwriter. The aim is to influence people. Scriptwriters and actors wish to obtain jobs from producers, and producers wish to obtain actors and scriptwriters to help with their productions (which must include actors).

Everyone has an action category, either Pursuer or Pursued. Do not play-act aggression or fear—the categories relate to the procedure for meetings. If you feel uncomfortable with your particular action category (or if you merely wish to try what it is like to be a Pursuer or Pursued), then try to find another person willing to swap categories or have a word with the facilitator.

ALPHA TELEVISION

Drama Department: Professional Activity

Head of Drama has agreed that not enough has been done in the past for our producers, scriptwriters and actors to meet together, to get to know each other better and to explore ideas for the benefit of our television drama.

Rather than have a 'just get on with it' meeting, we decided to add an extra ingredient—everyone has an action category and is either a Pursuer or a Pursued. All meetings must be between two people, never three or more.

1. Pursuers are the only people allowed to initiate a meeting.
2. Pursueds are the only people allowed to finish a meeting.
3. The Pursued spread themselves around the room and remain stationary until a Pursuer arrives and starts a meeting with them.
4. At the end of the meeting each Pursued has two options: (a) to leave the meeting and move elsewhere or (b) to continue the meeting for another couple of minutes. A Pursued cannot extend a meeting by longer than two minutes.

Do not spend too long with one person. Try to meet as many other people as possible, even those who are in the same job as yourself.

Job cards

Producer	Scriptwriter	Actor
Producer	Scriptwriter	Actor
Producer	Scriptwriter	Actor

Action cards

Pursuer	Pursued
Pursuer	Pursued
Pursuer	Pursued
Pursuer	Pursued
Pursuer	Pursued

25 Quality promotions

Description — A simulation about planning to grade staff by numbers to indicate quality and potential for promotion.

Objectives — To enhance the skills of creativity, communication, planning, presentation, teamwork and time management.

Time and numbers — With small numbers, the event might last for an hour. If there are large numbers, more time will be needed in the debriefing for explanations and comparisons and the event could take up to two hours. The minimum number is probably eight. There is no maximum number.

Resources
- Briefing sheet—one copy for each participant.
- Memo—one copy for each participant.
- Worksheet—one copy for each team.
- Scrap paper and perhaps aids to presentation—flipchart, overhead projector, etc.

Method
1. Hand out the Briefing sheets—one copy for each participant. Deal with the time-limits and the facilities for presentation.
2. Retrieve all the Briefing sheets. Fix two deadlines—the end of the planning period and the end of the presentation period.
3. Divide the participants into teams of between two and five and separate them as far as possible to reduce intrusive noise. If the numbers are sufficient, include a team representing the directors.
4. Hand out the Memo—one copy for each participant. Hand out the Worksheet—one copy for each team.
5. Make scrap paper available, plus any equipment for the presentations. If there is a management team, ask them to organize the facilities, including the order of presentation. Emphasize the requirement that teams keep to the deadlines.
6. Make sure that the arrangement of furniture for the presentations is appropriate. If participants simply remain in their groups and turn their chairs, the atmosphere is lacking in respect and professionalism and the simulation is lacking in credibility.

Debriefing

As everyone will have seen the presentations, it could be useful for each team (including directors) to give an account of their rejected ideas, mentioning the problems they faced and how they dealt with them. The debriefing will probably concentrate on the skills involved—creativity, communication, planning, presentation, teamwork and time management. For example, did teams concentrate so hard on their plan that they left little or no time to arrange for its presentation? Did they have a leader? Did they work out who should say what? Were individuals aware that their own careers could be affected, favourably or adversely, by the presentations?

Finally, is the idea of a Quality Number a viable idea?

Briefing

This is a simulation about planning to grade staff by numbers to indicate quality and potential for promotion.

You are on the staff of Alpha Household Enterprises, an organization which designs and manufactures a variety of household goods, including refrigerators, washing machines, dishwashers and microwaves. The company is particularly noted for its design work and is regarded as one of the most progressive and innovative in the Republic of Alpha.

Your task is explained in a Memo from the Board of Directors.

Alpha Household Enterprises

Inter-office Memorandum

From: Board of Directors

To: Executives

We require your cooperation in devising a new system for the promotion of staff.
   Under the present system all candidates for promotion go before an Appointments Board.
   The Board considers the performance of the candidate during the interview, plus a written report which is made by the candidate's superiors. The disadvantages are:

(a) Several staff who do not apply might do well in the job.
(b) The reports are based on a departmental perspective which may or may not reflect the interests of the company as a whole.
(c) The system gives too much weight to the views of each candidate's superiors.
(d) The interviews are snapshots of a particular candidate at a particular moment—and such a moment may be untypical and fail to take account of qualities and potential.

To meet some (or all) of these objections, we request that you draw up plans to give each member of staff a Quality Number—the number to be based on qualities and skills—and this number would be central to decisions on promotions.

1 Decide and list which qualities should be taken into account.
2 Decide how the qualities should be assessed.
3 Decide how many people (and which people) should allocate the Quality Numbers.
4 Decide on any other aspect which you feel needs to be addressed.

   Work in teams and fill in the Worksheet, which we shall study carefully during the coming weeks. Then present your plans verbally to us. We shall be looking for flair, lucidity and cooperation. We shall be favourably impressed if each member of a team says something during the presentation.
   We shall not be favourably impressed if some members of a team keep working on their plan after the deadline or fail to listen attentively to other teams' presentations.
   We hope you will find the tasks stimulating and enjoyable. We look forward to a creative result.

Alpha Household Enterprises

Worksheet

Team _____

Which qualities should be taken into account? _____
_____
_____
_____

How should the qualities be assessed? _____
_____
_____
_____

How many people (and which people) should allocate the Quality Numbers? _____
_____
_____
_____

What other factors need to be addressed? _____
_____
_____
_____

26 Rituals

Description | An exercise about devising and using rituals for meetings.

Objectives | To enhance the skills of creativity, communication and diplomacy in a situation which may involve aspects of gender and race. It could be used as an icebreaker.

Time and numbers | With small numbers the event might last for half an hour and, with larger numbers, the event can last up to an hour. The minimum number is probably five. There is no maximum number.

Resources
- Briefing sheet—one copy for each participant.
- Rituals form—one copy for each participant.
- Some device—whistle, buzzer, bell—for signalling the time-limits for meetings.

Method
1 Hand out the Briefing sheet—one copy to each participant—and discuss the facilities and time-limits—probably about five minutes for creating the original idea. Allow sufficient time during the action for everyone to meet everyone else.
2 Retrieve the Briefing sheets. Hand out the Rituals form—one copy to each participant. Set a deadline for each meeting and arrange a signal (buzzer, bell, whistle) to mark the time-limit for meetings.

Debriefing | The debriefing could begin with everyone remaining in place at the end of the action in their final pairs. The pairs could debrief themselves on their experiences. The pairs can then take it in turns to announce their findings, which could include comments on other people's rituals. The subsequent discussion could cover the issues that were raised—perhaps gender and race—and concentrate on the skills of creativity, communication and diplomacy. Finally, if the event was run as an icebreaker, how well did it work?

Briefing This is an exercise about devising and using rituals for meetings.

First, you create, individually and without consultation, a new ritual which could be used when meeting people. Write this at the top of your Rituals form. You then go round meeting other participants (in pairs, not threes or fours) and demonstrate your ritual. Comments on the other person's ritual should be written on the other person's Rituals form.

If you cannot think of a suitable ritual for a meeting, then interlock the fingers at chest height and explain that it is to express the hope of friendship and cooperation.

Rituals

Name ....

Ritual ....

....

Names	Comments

27 Selling art

Description A simulation involving artists, gallery owners and television journalists dealing with new works of art.

Objectives To enhance the skills of creativity, artistry, communication, diplomacy, negotiation, planning, presentation, teamwork and time management.

Time and numbers With small numbers the event might last for an hour, but with larger numbers, allow up to two hours. The minimum number is probably 12. There is no maximum number.

Resources
- Briefing sheet—one copy for each participant.
- Identity cards—three for the galleries, three for the television art programmes and a blank card for each artist.
- Television Schedule—one copy for the facilitator.
- Scrap paper, including some large sheets and coloured pens.
- A box of everyday objects which artists can use—perhaps containing paper cups, scissors, fruit, old magazines, paper-clips, rulers, nails, soap, plasticine, etc.

Method
1. It could be useful to allocate the roles randomly in advance of the event, giving participants time to create their works or to draw up plans for exhibiting or televising. With 12 participants there could be six artists, three gallery owners and three television art reporters from the three channels. With more participants, there can be teams representing the galleries and the television teams.
2. Hand out the Briefing sheets and the identity cards. Discuss the facilities that are available and arrange for deadlines. Allocate a base for each artist, each gallery and each television programme.
3. Explain your own position as facilitating the television broadcasts. For example, they cannot start haphazardly, they must be scheduled. Display the Television Schedule. Retrieve all the Briefing sheets and make sure that working surfaces are cleared of any non-authentic clutter.
4. Make scrap paper available, including some large sheets and coloured pens.
5. Try to smooth the action and avoid delays.

Debriefing

This could start with the participants getting together with their colleagues and debriefing themselves—all the artists in one group, the gallery owners in another and the television reporters in a third group. They can then take it in turns to report their findings and experiences. The discussion can then go down an appropriate road, but would presumably cover the skills involved.

Briefing

This is a simulation in which art galleries, artists and television art magazine journalists deal in works of art related to any everyday object or a combined group of objects (paper cups, scissors, pens, etc.).

The action takes place in the Republic of Alpha where the Ministry of Arts is sponsoring New Art Week, to be devoted to 'new works of art related to everyday life'.

The three main commercial galleries—Look Gallery, Vision Gallery and Behold Gallery—wish to feature at least two works of art each.

The three main television channels—Alpha 1, Alpha 2 and Alpha 3—hope to produce at least two broadcasts each featuring the work of one or more artists. These broadcasts could be in the studio or in an art gallery.

Each artist will produce one work of art and hope to have it exhibited in a gallery and also featured on television. Artists should write their names on their identity cards.

Television broadcasts are scheduled so that the three channels do not overlap their art programmes. The starting and finishing deadlines for each broadcast are very important. Any overrunning and the artist, art gallery owner or presenter might be chopped off mid-sentence to allow the next programme to start on time.

No work, no discussions and no demonstrations can take place during a television broadcast. All non-participants must be the television audience and watch silently.

Identity cards

Look Gallery	VISION GALLERY	**Behold Gallery**
Alpha 1	Alpha 2	ALPHA 3
.... Artist	.... Artist	.... Artist
.... Artist	.... Artist	.... Artist

Television schedules

Channel	Starting time	Finishing time	Description of programme

28 Skills alone

Description A simulation about job interviews relating to qualities rather than specific jobs.

Objectives To enhance the skills of creativity, communication, diplomacy and teamwork.

Time and numbers With small numbers the event might last for an hour, but with larger numbers, allow more than an hour. The minimum number is probably eight. There is no maximum number.

Resources
- Briefing sheet—one copy for each participant.
- Profiles for four companies.
- Profiles for four candidates.
- Scrap paper.

Method
1 Hand out the Briefing sheets and discuss the facilities, particularly the arrangement of the furniture.
2 Fix a time-limit for each session of interviews.
3 Allocate roles at random—perhaps by placing the Profiles face down and allowing participants to pick their own. With more than eight participants, the company representatives can be expanded to two or three per team.
4 Retrieve all the Briefing sheets and arrange the furniture so that each company has sufficient room and freedom from noisy distractions. Make scrap paper available.

Debriefing It could be useful for companies and candidates to take it in turns to relate their experiences. The general discussion might cover the question of whether job selection by skills alone was viable or fair. However, the main discussion is likely to be the skills—creativity, communication, diplomacy and teamwork.

Briefing

This is a simulation of a series of job interviews in which job applicants each have four differently ranked skills—talking, inventing, organizing and analysing.

There are four computer software manufacturers, each with different problems and each seeking suitable candidates to help tackle those problems.

All interviews must start with the companies showing their Profiles and the candidates showing their skills Profiles. The object is to find a match where the candidate could help the company.

The discussion must be on skills alone. Experience is not required, except to the extent that all candidates have the necessary experience—the question is the level of skill. So if you are a candidate, do not invent a background of experience—'I was top programmer at Alpha Computers'.

Jobs must not be offered, nor should there be any discussion of such matters as salaries and promotion opportunities. The interviews are exploratory only—any decisions will take place in the days to follow.

It is important that interviews should end on time. If you wish to take a short break to collect your thoughts, then end an interview early.

Company profiles

ALPHA COMPUTERS

Our problems are muddled filing systems and poor staff relations

ALPHA SOFTWARE

Our problems are out-of-date products and too many staff

Alpha Networks

Our problems are lack of motivation and poor career prospects

Alpha Systems

Our problems are poor publicity and a discontented sales department

Candidate profiles

CANDIDATE A

My order of skills: 1 communicating, 2 planning, 3 creating, 4 negotiating.

CANDIDATE B

My order of skills: 1 planning, 2 creating, 3 negotiating, 4 communicating.

CANDIDATE C

My order of skills: 1 creating, 2 negotiating, 3 communicating, 4 planning.

CANDIDATE D

My order of skills: 1 negotiating, 2 communicating, 3 planning, 4 creating.

29 Sleeping Beauty

Description A simulation in which Sleeping Beauty, the King and Queen, the Prince, the Witch and Anon meet advocates (lawyers) and scribes (authors and journalists).

Objectives To enhance the skills of creativity, communication, diplomacy, negotiation, planning and teamwork.

Time and numbers With small numbers the event might last for an hour, but with larger numbers, allow up to two hours. The minimum number is probably eight. There is no maximum number.

Resources
- Briefing sheet—one copy for each participant.
- Article in *Alpha History Journal*.
- Identity cards—one for each participant (eight roles).
- Scrap paper.

Method
1 Hand out the Briefing sheets.
2 Allocate roles at random, perhaps by placing the Identity cards face down and allowing the participants to pick their own. With large numbers, there could either be an increase in the number of scribes and advocates or the simulation could be run as two separate events.
3 Arrange the furniture so that it is appropriate. If there is a superior location, it should be given to the King and Queen. Retrieve the Briefing sheets.
4 Set a deadline for the end of the event. During the action, facilitate any public activity—for example, someone might request facilities to give a news conference or make a Royal Proclamation.

Debriefing It could be useful for participants to take it in turns to reveal what happened and report any differences between their motives ('I want to make money') and their words ('I want to give you a chance to tell your side of the story'). Once the facts have been established, the debriefing can go down appropriate roads, including an assessment of the various skills—communication, diplomacy, planning—used by the participants.

Briefing

The real story of The Sleeping Beauty of Alpha is referred to in a recent article in the *Alpha History Journal*, the journal of the Alpha History Association. You will receive a copy of this together with your role. The roles are King, Queen, Beauty, Prince, Witch, Anon, advocates (lawyers) and scribes (journalists and authors).

Your job is to do your duty to the Kingdom and, if possible, enhance your fame and wealth. Do not play-act your role—just behave professionally. The gender of the role should not affect your decision-making—simply do what seems to be in the interests of the person concerned.

If you wish to initiate a public event (a Royal Proclamation, a legal move, a publicity event), then you must consult the facilitator to arrange a time and an attentive audience. All participants must watch all public events.

Regarding the law, although witchcraft is no longer a crime kidnapping is a crime, and there could be civil actions for damage, loss of earnings, damage for libel and slander, etc. All agreements between parties are legally binding, whether verbal or written, but written agreements are safer.

ALPHA HISTORY JOURNAL

The Real Story of Sleeping Beauty

by J. A. H. Arlinga FAHA

The real story of Sleeping Beauty is contained in the manuscript[1] by Anon[2] the King's scribe, now in the library of the Old Royal Palace in Alpha. It is significantly different from the fairy story concocted several hundred years later.

The manuscript contains no 'wicked fairy', but there is a witch. Anon calls her a 'wicked witch', but she strongly denied that she was wicked. However, as Feydoran (1992) has pointed out, witchcraft was abolished as a crime several years earlier by Royal Proclamation on the grounds that it was all superstition with no basis in fact.

Unlike the fairy story, there was no spell which 'froze' the whole court for a hundred years. What happened was that a wealthy baron appeared as a suitor for the hand of Beauty but, as he was old and of somewhat repulsive appearance, Beauty pleaded with her father and mother that she should not be made to marry him. The King and Queen were undecided and at this point two things happened simultaneously. A self-styled witch, who specialized in love potions and healing medicines, cast a spell, saying that 'The Princess will sleep without love'. This was widely publicized throughout the Kingdom and enhanced the reputation of the witch in the eyes of many of the subjects. Immediately after the casting of the spell Beauty fell asleep[3] for five days and five nights. A visiting Prince was allowed to the bedside and kissed[4] Beauty, who awoke, and since the Prince was rich, which satisfied the King and Queen, and was handsome in Beauty's eyes, the two married and lived happily together.

One immediate consequence of Anon's work was that copies were made by employees of Anon and the Kingdom gained from an increase in tourism[5].

Notes

1 The manuscript is written on parchment in beautiful Ancient Alpha script.
2 It is not known whether Anon was male or female. Most authorities have assumed that Anon was male. However, Feydoran's recent *History of Ancient Alpha* puts forward the possibility that Anon was female.
3 An authoritative medical historian (Krausner, 1986) suggests that this was almost certainly a coma.
4 It may not have been an actual kiss. In translation the word is also used for a caress. (See Hursentz, Mariotti and Braque, *Alpha Language Analysis*, 1956.)
5 See *Tourism in Alpha as influenced by Literature, Myth, Magic and Legend* (Cottens and Hubbard, 1985).

Identity cards

King	Queen
Beauty	Prince
Witch	Anon
scribe	advocate
scribe	advocate

30 Spaceship Peace

Description
: A simulation about a spaceship for peace which runs out of food and visits Earth.

Objectives
: To enhance the skills of creativity, communication, diplomacy, negotiation, planning, presentation, teamwork and time management in a situation involving aspects of race. There is a hidden agenda—the Earthlings are unaware of the particular needs of the Peacelanders.

Time and numbers
: With small numbers the event might last for an hour but, with larger numbers, allow up to two hours. The minimum number is probably eight. There is no maximum number.

Resources
:
- Briefing sheet—one copy for each participant.
- Space Order P317—one copy for each Peacelander.
- Space Divisional Commanders—four profiles: Culture, Economics, Ethics and Security.
- Security Council Resolution 2131—one copy for each Earthling.
- Earth's Regional Negotiators—four background briefings: Africa, America, Asia, Europe.
- Two rooms are desirable.
- Scrap paper.

Method
: (*Note*: It may not be advisable to run this event with participants who are unduly sensitive.)

   1. Hand out the Briefing sheets—one copy for each participant. Discuss the facilities and set a time-limit for the joint meeting. If two rooms are not available, perhaps the Peacelanders could meet in a corridor (canteen, library, etc.) as it is very important that the Earthlings should not overhear what the Peacelanders are saying nor catch a glimpse of their private documents.
   2. Retrieve the Briefing sheets and make scrap paper available.
   3. Divide randomly and then separate the two groups into two different areas (rooms).
   4. Hand out the secret documents to each group, making quite sure that

neither side sees the other's documents. With each side there is one main document and four individual documents. Cut out these individual documents and hand them at random to the appropriate sub-groups of Peacelanders or Earthlings.

5 With more than eight participants, you could arrange for one or two volunteers to help you run the event, or add an extra person (assistant) to one of the individual roles. With fewer than eight participants, it could be possible for one person to take on two roles.

Debriefing

The first step should be to disclose the secret documents—the simplest way is to pass them all over to the other group. If this is not done, unjustified suspicions may arise but not be made public because people may be too polite to say such things as 'I think you may have lied to us'. In this debriefing openness is vital.

The next step follows naturally—for each side to reveal their plans. For example, the Peacelanders may have decided that the best way to break the bad news was to go into the meeting not as a group but as individuals, hoping to make friends and influence people before revealing their needs. Ask the participants to reveal their secret thoughts, hopes, motives, suspicions.

The general discussion could cover the specific circumstances of the event and move on to the general aspects of breaking bad news. This also relates to the specific skills—diplomacy, communication, creativity, negotiation, planning, presentation, teamwork and time management. Also, depending on the interests of the participants, the questions of race (or species) can be discussed together with ethics. The question could be put: How important is a human life in relation to the lives of other species in distant galaxies?

Briefing

It is 10 years into the future. Spaceship Peace has arrived off Earth and is halfway on its voyage to bring peace to the Five Planets of the Hexto Galaxy. It is in urgent need of food. The refrigeration system failed at the precise moment that the back-up system was off-line for servicing. All faults have been rectified, but the food was destroyed.

Earth has agreed in principle to supply food and a meeting will take place at the headquarters of the United Nations. The Earthlings will be represented by negotiators from the Big Four regions—Africa, America, Asia and Europe. The Peacelanders will be represented by the four officers in charge of Culture, Economics, Ethics and Security.

Neither side at the negotiating table can declare or start a war—the only action available is to make recommendations (which could include a joint agreement) to be passed on to the Space Command Council of the spaceship and to the Regional Governments of Earth. All are negotiators, not commanders.

The Peacelanders have monitored Earth and are familiar with its customs and conditions.

The only facts are those contained in the documents, but you can assume that Earth is much the same as it is today, apart from the regrouping of countries into regions. Each side will have private documents explaining the situation as known to that side.

The event is in three stages: (1) both sides meet separately and privately, (2) both sides meet together and (3) both sides again meet separately and privately.

You are a negotiator—either a Peacelander or an Earthling. Do not play-act. Whether you are an Earthling or a Peacelander behave professionally, accept your responsibilities and do your duty.

SPACE CONTROL COMMAND

Space Order P317

To: The Officers of Security, Economics, Culture and Ethics

Our scientists inform us, with the greatest regret, that the only food Earth possesses which can sustain life is Earthlings themselves. We need 1 000 000 (one million) human beings, in good condition. Other potential sources of food—animals, vegetables, fruit, fish, etc.—have been carefully examined but, although these could be eaten without harm, they would not sustain life.

1. *Try to persuade the Earthling representatives to provide us with one million human beings in good condition.*

2. *Operate within Space Order X2-5:*

    'The mission is to create a lasting peace among the five planets of Hexto Galaxy and no action must be taken which is contrary to this order.'

In exchange for the food we can offer only the promise of future cooperation with Earth, which could occur in about 100 Earth years. Since Spaceship Peace is not a trading vessel it has only 'Mission Required' items and these cannot be given away. The honour of the Peacelander Mission is at stake. Any negotiator who promises what cannot be delivered will be severely punished.

Space Command: Officer of Culture

Earthlings are bitterly divided over culture and race. Although most Earthlings state that all human beings are equal, in practice many races and religions regard themselves as superior to other races and religions. This division may create opportunities to negotiate with individual regions.

Space Command: Officer of Economics

Food is an economic resource and vital to the mission. Earthlings have a high emotional factor, which will probably lead to them refusing our request for food. However, economically the benefits of supplying us with food would benefit not only ourselves but also millions of beings in Hexto Galaxy. From Earth's point of view, the provision of the food would help to remove some of the economic problems caused by over-population, particularly in Asia.

Space Command: Officer of Ethics

Earthlings are noted for greed, selfishness and occasional cruelty. Unlike Peacelanders, some Earthlings gain pleasure from the suffering of others. Unlike Peacelanders, who make sure that food is kept in pleasant conditions, the Earthlings frequently keep food in revolting and painful conditions. Unlike Peacelanders, some Earthlings hunt and kill animals for sport and pleasure.

Space Command: Officer of Security

The missile deflectors are automatic. Any hostile missile is automatically jammed and redirected to its point of origin. This system cannot be overridden.

If weaponry is required to secure our necessary food requirements, the most efficient instrument is the Brain Ray which paralyses but does not kill. The effects wear off after several hours. There would be no problem in applying the Brain Ray to a large city, such as New York, London, Paris, Delhi, Tokyo, Cairo, etc., and collection of food can then progress easily by means of cargo shuttle.

Security Council Emergency Resolution 2131

Under the terms of Emergency Resolution 2131 the Security Council has set up a Four-Region Delegation to:

- discuss among themselves what foods might be available for the Peacelanders;

- find out from the Peacelanders if they require any special type of food;

- make recommendations to the United Nations and/or specific Governments on what action should be taken;

- discuss any related matters, including the countries which would supply the food and the apportionment of costs.

Note: According to the latest figures available, the wealth of the world (as measured by Gross National Product) is as follows:

Africa	2 per cent
America	47 per cent
Asia	14 per cent
Europe	37 per cent
Total	100 per cent

Africa: Background briefing

Although Africa has the least wealth of the four regions, it is willing to supply any specialized food that is needed—for example, if elephants are the main food. However, the costs involved would, in the opinion of the countries of the area, best be met by the humanitarian aid from the wealthier regions. On this basis, Africa would have little stake in the outcome and, therefore, the African negotiator would have the impartiality needed if the negotiators were to choose a leader and this point should be considered.

✂--

America: Background briefing

America includes some of the poorest countries of the world with undeveloped infrastructure. So, although the United States would be in a good position to assist if the Peacelanders required cattle or grain, the situation would not be so easy if the food were exotic species. The region is prepared to pay 47 per cent of the total cost of the whole operation, including compensation for those adversely affected. Since the region is willing to pay the largest part of the bill, the American negotiator would be willing, if desired, to take on the role of chief negotiator.

✂--

Asia: Background briefing

Although Asia includes one or two of the wealthiest countries of the world, the general position is that of developing economies, difficult terrain and inadequate transport to cover the sort of food collection and transportation that might be necessary. If the food required were rice or bamboo there would be no major problems apart from harvesting and transport, but it would not be in a position to supply any significant amounts of meat. Regarding finance, the region is a developing one and, therefore, it would be in the interest of the world economy as a whole if total costs were met by America and Europe. On the question of a possible leader of the negotiators, the skills of negotiation are very important in Asian culture and should not be neglected.

✂--

Europe: Background briefing

Although, according to the latest statistics, Europe represents 37 per cent of the world's wealth, it produces far less than 37 per cent of the world's food supplies. While Europe could supply cattle and dairy produce, it could not supply much in the way of wild animals, or rice, mangoes, coconuts, etc. It is willing to supply advanced technology for other regions to harvest, collect or transport the goods required. Any central collection area would best be located in areas of great land mass, such as Africa or Asia. Europe would be willing to bear 37 per cent of the total cost of the operation, including the costs relating to advice, computer technology, and so on. Regarding negotiations, Europe—by history and experience—has a world outlook and therefore would be willing to assume the role of chief negotiator if this were thought desirable.

31 Stupidity Bills

Description — A simulation in which Members of Parliament seek to legislate against stupidity.

Objectives — To enhance the skills of creativity, communication, negotiation, planning, presentation and teamwork.

Time and numbers — With small numbers the event might last for an hour but, with larger numbers, allow up to two hours. The minimum number is probably eight. There is no maximum number.

Resources
- Briefing sheet—one copy for each participant.
- Alpha Environment Party document—one copy for each participant.
- Suggestions and Comments form—one copy for each group.
- Scrap paper.

Method
1. Hand out the Briefing sheets, discuss the facilities and announce a time for the beginning of the joint meeting of all participants.
2. Retrieve all the Briefing sheets and hand out the Alpha Environment Party document—one copy for each participant. With luck, the participants will divide themselves into random groups, but if this seems unlikely to happen, group them randomly in teams of between two and five people.
3. Hand out the Suggestions and Comments form—one copy to each group.
4. Make scrap paper available.
5. If there are sufficient numbers, one person or group can take the role of senior Party MPs to supervise the proceedings and take charge of the joint meeting.

Debriefing — It may be a good idea to allow everyone to take it in turns to express, briefly, their own thoughts and feelings about the event and reveal private discussions within groups. The debriefing could then consider not only the general question of stupidity and legislation but also the skills involved during the event. For example, to what extent did teams organize themselves for the presentation of their ideas or did they merely ignore the problem and leave it to the extroverts to give their versions?

Briefing

This is a simulation in which Members of Parliament seek to legislate against stupidity. You are either a member of the Environment Party in Alpha or a friendly member of Alpha University who has been invited to join in group discussions and give advice. If, in real life, you are an expert (or are knowledgeable) in any relevant field (law, psychology, sociology, etc.), consider taking the role of a Professor of that subject.

The event is in two stages—small group discussions followed by a joint meeting. You will all receive an explanatory document from the Environment Party relating to the session, plus a form which can be filled in giving suggestions and comments.

Alpha Environment Party

The Leaders of the Alpha Environment Party thank Environment MPs and academics from Alpha University for attending. We should be grateful if you would divide randomly into pairs or trios, address the following problems, and then announce your findings to the meeting as a whole. No specific decisions are required at this time, we are merely exploring options.

Background

As part of our election promises we undertook to introduce specific legislation to curb human error in economic decision-making—what the media have called the Stupidity Bills. Stupidity is enormously costly in money, resources and human suffering. It damages the health and well-being of the nation in many ways. While we have our own ideas on possible legislation we would be most interested to learn your views.

Objectives

If we are able to identify, deter and even punish stupidity, it would not only be of enormous benefit to Alpha in human and material terms, it would also give Alpha a significant trade advantage over most other countries where stupidity is rife, unchecked and often concealed by cover-ups, bribery and corruption.

Action

To provide at least the outline of legislation, including:

1 The name of the Bill (or Bills) to be placed before Parliament.
2 A brief preamble to give the objectives.
3 A definition of stupidity.
4 The issue of the concealment of stupidity.
5 The type of penalties to be imposed.
6 Which types of stupidity should be exempt from the legislation.

Suggestions and comments

Names of members of the group ....

....

Suggestions, comments ....

....

....

....

....

....

....

....

....

....

....

....

32 Television Kitchen

Description	A simulation with roles for a TV company and groups of cookery school staff.
Objectives	To enhance the skills of creativity, communication, planning, presentation, teamwork and time management.
Time and numbers	With small numbers the event might last for an hour but, with larger numbers, allow up to two hours. The minimum number is probably eight. There is no maximum number.
Resources	• Briefing sheet—one copy for each participant. • Alpha 4 Instructions—one copy for each participant. • Scrap paper, including large sheets of paper and coloured pens. • A table is required for the demonstrations, and if there is no clock in the room a small one should be provided.
Method	1 Hand out the Briefing sheets and discuss facilities, including the furniture and the location for the demonstrations. 2 The size of the teams will depend on numbers and the time available. With eight participants there could be three cookery teams and one television team—each with two participants. The cookery teams could be allocated colours—green team, purple team, etc. Set a deadline for the beginning of the presentations. 3 Retrieve the Briefing sheets and hand out the Alpha 4 Instructions—one copy to each participant. 4 Make scrap paper available, plus some large sheets of paper and coloured pens. 5 During the presentations it could increase authenticity to have a coloured card to represent each team. However, the TV team should be in charge of arrangements and should say a few words at the end of all the demonstrations, even if it is only 'Thank you, we will let you know the result by next week'.
Debriefing	Each team could begin by debriefing themselves—discussing the skills they used, the problems they met and how they tackled the problems,

including rejected ideas. When teams, including the TV team, have explained what happened in their territory the discussion could cover the quality of the skills of presentations, plus the other skills used—creativity, communication, planning, teamwork and time management. The subsequent discussion could cover the problems and opportunities of cookery on television, perhaps using examples of what happened during the event.

Briefing

This is a simulation about Alpha 4 Television auditioning groups of cookery school staff for the job of running a television cookery series. You are either on one of the cookery school teams or you are on the staff of Alpha 4 Television supervising the auditions.

You will have a document—Instructions to cookery teams—which explains the situation.

Alpha 4

Instructions to Cookery Teams

Thank you for applying for the project to run a series of cookery programmes on Alpha 4.

As you already know, when the station opened last year an independent company produced a series of programmes entitled Master Cook.

Neither the title nor the contents turned out to be entirely satisfactory. The major complaint was that the dishes illustrated were far too complicated, contained far too many ingredients and were too 'French' rather than dealing with the more homely cooking of Alpha.

We therefore wish to start a new series aimed at the average viewer—not only those who can already cook to a reasonable standard but those who have only a vague and often mistaken view of basic techniques. Just to give one example, a recent survey of a television audience at a cookery programme revealed that only 10 per cent knew the most effective technique to chop an onion.

Our provisional title for the new series is Television Kitchen—but please come up with a different title if you find one which is more suitable for your ideas. Use large sheets of paper if you wish to illustrate large ideas.

You are not expected to produce a complete programme. What we would like to see is the overall plan plus a snippet of how part of one programme might appear to viewers. Any props must be imaginary, so you could refer to 'This mixing bowl (this orange, oven, salt, etc.)'.

Since timing is vital in television, we shall expect you to end your demonstration on time. You could underrun by a minute or so, but if you overrun by as much as one second we will not be favourably impressed. Also, please respect other teams and watch in silence during their demonstrations.

Although we may comment immediately after your demonstrations, no final decisions will be reached until we have viewed the recordings and discussed in detail the work of the teams.

33 Training methods

Description
: A simulation about devising plans for assessing and improving training.

Objectives
: To enhance the skills of creativity, communication, diplomacy, presentation and teamwork.

Time and numbers
: With small numbers, the event might last for half an hour. If there are several events run in parallel, more time will be needed in the debriefing for explanation, comparisons and comments and the event could take about an hour. The minimum number is probably six. There is no maximum number.

Resources
: - Briefing sheet—one copy for each participant.
  - Candidates' Assessment—one copy for each participant.
  - Proposal Form—one copy for each candidate (half the number of participants).
  - Research Paper—one copy for each participant.
  - Small clocks—a possibility for each Deputy Editor if there is no clock in the room(s).
  - It may be an advantage to have more than one room to ensure privacy and freedom from noisy distractions.
  - Scrap paper.

Method
: 1 Hand out the Briefing sheets—one copy for each participant.
  2 Discuss the facilities and set a time-limit for the start of the interviews and also the length of each interview. Discuss how to allocate the roles of candidate and 'reference library'—should pairs decide between themselves which should be the candidate and which the 'reference library', or should it be done at random?
  3 The arrangement of furniture for the work on the Proposal might be different from the interviews—the first might have pairs sitting side by side while the interviewing could be face-to-face across a table. Space the furniture so that pairs can talk privately and without noisy distractions.
  4 Retrieve the Briefing sheets and divide the participants at random into pairs.

5 Hand out the Candidates' Assessment—one to each participant.
6 Hand out the Research Paper—one to each participant (including the 'reference library' person).
7 Hand out the Proposal Form—one copy for the candidate in each pair.
8 Make scrap paper available.
9 Make sure that the deadlines are strictly observed.

Debriefing   This could begin with participants taking it in turns to give a brief account of their experiences, both in the first half and the second half of the event. The discussion will probably concentrate on the skills involved—creativity, communication, diplomacy, presentation and teamwork. However, it could also cover the wider question of training methodology and deal with some of the issues raised in the Research Paper.

Briefing

This is a simulation about devising plans for assessing and improving training.

A new glossy magazine, *Alpha Training Methods*, is about to be published and the magazine is holding an assessment session with candidates for full-time (or part-time) jobs as writers of articles on training. In the first part of the task the candidates are to produce the outline of an article based on an academic research report and in the second part the Deputy Editors interview the applicants on the basis of their outlines.

In the first part of the simulation you meet privately in pairs—one person being in the role of candidate and the other in the role of a 'reference library'. The reference library person observes the progress of the article and supplies 'facts' on request. For example, the candidate might wish to know how many large companies there are in the Republic of Alpha, or whether it is intended that the magazine should aim to be international.

The candidate should not ask questions such as 'What do you think of this headline?', nor should the reference library person answer such questions. Opinions must not be given. The facts provided by (invented by) the reference library should be as plausible as possible.

In the second part of the simulation the reference library persons become Deputy Editors and interview the candidates. They should not interview the candidate they were paired with unless they have interviewed all the other candidates.

The interviews must concentrate entirely on the article itself. You can assume that questions relating to any former journalistic experience or qualifications have already been covered and that questions relating to rates of pay, conditions of work and the like will be dealt with at subsequent interviews with appropriate staff.

You will receive a document—'Candidates' Assessment'—explaining the nature of the task, plus a copy of a research paper in an academic journal. Candidates (but not reference library people) will have a Proposal Form, to be filled in by the candidate to indicate the thrust of the proposed article.

Alpha Training Methods

Candidates' Assessment

The assessment is in two halves.

First produce the outline of an article based on a research paper by Hilliard, Cord and Feckley. Use the Proposal Form. We want (a) the main headline, (b) a second headline and (c) about 20 words which can be featured in a 'box'. If you contemplate using any reference library facts in your article, mention these facts briefly at the bottom of your form.

A full article is NOT required and must NOT be attempted.

In the second part of the assessment you will be interviewed on a one-to-one basis by several of our Deputy Editors in order that we can have the benefit of separate opinions of your work. The interviews will give you a chance to show your outline and discuss it with the Deputy Editors. No other questions will arise, so the Deputy Editors will not be asking you about your journalistic or managerial experience. All of you have adequate experience, so please do not raise this issue or any other matters unconnected with the proposed article.

To avoid candidates having to wait their turn to be interviewed, all interviews must end on time, or can end before time if you would like a short break to collect your thoughts.

Best of luck, and we hope you enjoy the task.

Alpha Training Methods

Proposal

Name of candidate ....

Main headline ....

Second headline ....

Text for box (no more than 20 words) ....

....

....

....

Reference facts ....

....

....

....

....

....

....

....

....

Research Paper

Methodological Differences in Training in Alpha

by Hilliard, P., Cord, F. G. and Feckley, W. R.

Summary

Our research study compares the usage of two methodologies—Instruction and Autonomy—in the training departments of nearly 100 large companies in Alpha. Our findings reveal significant differences of usage. We conclude that further research should be carried out, to be funded by both private and public organizations.

Objectives

The aims of our research were to find out if there were any significant differences in the popularity of different training techniques. We concentrated our research on two very different training approaches which, for the sake of simplicity, we have called Instruction and Autonomy.

Definitions

We define Instruction as those techniques in which the instructor directly instructs the trainees—whether by the spoken or written word, or by video or computer programs. We define Autonomy as those techniques where the instructor gives autonomy to the trainees to elicit answers, take decisions and initiate action, usually in a structured context such as simulations, exercises, games and role-plays.

Procedures

We obtained a list of companies in Alpha who employ more than 200 staff. We selected 100 of these companies at random and sent their training departments a short and simple questionnaire.

The questionnaire first gave our definition of Instruction and Autonomy and then asked several questions to find out to what extent the training involved these two methods. For example, the first question was 'Do you personally use one specific method of teaching, or do you use a mixture of methods?'

Results

We received a high level of response—96 companies completed the questionnaire. Of these 96 responses, 2 per cent said they used the Autonomy Method all the time and another 9 per cent said they used the Autonomy Method most of the time, making a total of 11 per cent. This was in sharp contrast with the numbers using the Instructional Method. Of the 96 replies, some 71 per cent said they used the Instructional Method all the time and 13 per cent said they used it most of the time, making a total of 84 per cent. A handful of responses indicated that the training department could give no firm figures, as their instructors used whichever method seemed

(Continued)

appropriate for the occasion. One reply which was more specific said, 'Some of my sessions start with instruction, include autonomy and finish with instruction, so I cannot give you any useful figures'.

From personal observation we were sometimes puzzled by an apparent difference between what was said and what was done. For example, in one session at a large company the activity was called a 'game', which the trainer categorized as Autonomy, but in practice the instructor allowed virtually no autonomy and was constantly telling the trainees what they should do. If this misunderstanding occurred to any significant degree in the sample, it would mean that the use of Instructional methodology is even greater than the above figures suggest.

Conclusions

We conclude that Instructional training is widespread and that there is some confusion about methodological terminology. We recommend that a further study be made to see (a) whether the use of the Instructional method is increasing or decreasing, (b) the reason for any increase or decrease, (c) whether Government training policy should offer directives on methods and (d) whether there is a case for providing better (or more varied) training for the trainers.

We further recommend that any further studies should be large-scale, should include small as well as large companies and that the findings should be based on personal inspection of training sessions by experienced observers rather than by relying solely on the findings of questionnaires. In view of the national (and international) importance of training, we suggest that both public and private bodies be approached to fund the research.

34 Typists' veto

Description   A simulation involving plans to give Typists the power of veto on letters and documents.

Objectives   To enhance the skills of creativity, communication, diplomacy, planning and teamwork in a situation which might involve aspects of gender or race.

Time and numbers   With small numbers, the event might last for half an hour. If there are several events run in parallel, more time will be needed in the debriefing for explanation and comments and the event could take about an hour. The minimum number is probably six. There is no maximum number.

Resources
- Briefing sheet—one copy for each participant.
- Memo—one copy for each participant.
- Job cards—one (of two) for each participant.
- Ideas sheet—one for each participant.
- Scrap paper.

Method
1. Hand out the Briefing sheets and discuss the facilities, including the arrangement of the furniture to secure reasonable privacy for the individual meetings followed by moving the chairs and tables to suit a joint meeting. Fix a time-limit for the start of the joint meeting.
2. Retrieve the Briefing sheets and distribute the Job cards at random, with the same number of Typists as executives. This could be done by turning the cards face down and allowing participants to pick their own.
3. Hand out the Memo and also the Ideas sheet, one of each to each participant.
4. Make scrap paper available.

Debriefing   Participants could take it in turns to describe how well (or badly) the executives and Typists cooperated and to reveal any secret thoughts or plans. The debriefing could then turn to the skills involved—creativity, communication, diplomacy, planning and teamwork—based on examples of what happened during the event. The general discussion could cover the question of responsibility. For example, should only the managers manage? If, during the event, participants envisaged that most Typists were likely to be female and/or from ethnic minorities, then aspects of gender and race might be discussed.

Briefing   This is a simulation involving plans to give Typists the power of veto on letters and documents. You are either a Typist or an executive in the company Finance & Trading Enterprises in the Republic of Alpha. You will receive a memo from your boss explaining the situation. You will also receive an Ideas sheet to jot down ideas, plans and recommendations.

Finance & Trading Enterprises

MEMO

From: Managing Director

To: Executives and Typists

I have been giving some thought to ways in which efficiency could be improved and morale raised.

As you know, when I took over the ownership of the company last month following the death of my father, I had already spent several months in the job of typist. During that time I became most impressed by the honesty, intelligence and dedication of non-executive staff, who often spotted mistakes, gave advice, and yet were sometimes ignored or treated with condescension.

As you know, I do not believe in huge reorganizations. I prefer training staff to dismissing staff. I wish to see more humanity in office life. Consequently, I want each executive to pair with a typist to discuss the possibility of introducing what I might call a Typists' veto. By that I mean that no letter or document would be authorized unless approved by the typist. Executives would still take decisions but typists could block action.

Please meet in pairs—one typist and one executive in each pair—and put forward ideas about the benefits which might be gained and any possible disadvantages.

Write your name at the top of your Ideas sheet and fill it in individually—although you can consult with the other member of your pair. You do not have to answer the questions and you may wish to raise other matters. That is entirely up to you. I look forward to reading your thoughts on the subject.

After meeting in pairs, please form into a single group and see if any of the ideas can be generally accepted. I hope that we can all make useful progress towards a more efficient, cooperative and humanitarian office.

Finance & Trading Enterprises

Ideas

Name _____ Status _____

What advantages and disadvantages do you see in a Typists' veto? _____
_____
_____
_____

What should be the procedure when a Typist vetoes a letter or document? _____
_____
_____
_____

Should Typists be part of the process of selection and promotion within the company? _____
_____
_____
_____

Any other comments? _____
_____
_____
_____

Job cards

Executive	Typist
Executive	Typist
Executive	Typist
Executive	Typist
Executive	Typist
Executive	Typist

35 Virus X

Description A simulation about an isolated group trying to survive a natural disaster.

Objectives To enhance the skills of creativity, communication, planning, teamwork and time management.

Time and numbers With small numbers, the event might last for half an hour. If there are several events run in parallel, more time will be needed in the debriefing for explanation and comments and the event could take about an hour. The minimum number is probably five. There is no maximum number.

Resources
- Briefing sheet—one copy for each participant.
- Our List—one copy for each participant.
- Our History—one copy for each participant.
- Scrap paper.

Method
1. Hand out the Briefing sheets—one for each participant—and discuss the arrangement of the furniture. Ideally it should be movable to allow the participants to form groups of whatever size they wish and in whatever location seems appropriate. Set a deadline for the end of the event.
2. Retrieve the Briefing sheets and remove any clutter which looks survival-like (sandwiches, coffee, portable telephones).
3. Hand out Our History and Our List—one copy of each for each participant. Make scrap paper available.

Debriefing The format of the debriefing could depend on how the participants organized themselves. If they split into pairs, it could be useful for each pair to relate what happened but, if they operated as a single committee, there would be no need for such disclosure, except perhaps individuals revealing any secret thoughts, for example, 'How I tried to become leader'. If you run this event several times, or if the participants divide into groups, a wide variety of plans may emerge. Tin lids could be nailed to the roof as a sign if the helicopter returned. The nails and wire could be made into a radio. The books could be burned—but what about the children? The tarpaulin (and perhaps some of the linoleum) could become a tent for warmth.

Part of the debriefing could focus on the skills—creativity, communication, planning, teamwork and time management. Time management is important because the participants could decide on immediate action as well as talk: 'Facilitator, two of us are nailing the tin lids to the roof right now and spelling out the letters H E L P'.

Briefing

This is a simulation about an isolated group trying to survive a natural disaster in the mountain country in the Republic of Alpha. The disaster which has hit Alpha, and perhaps many other countries, is known as the Virus X.

The survivors are in a single-room schoolhouse. Most are adults, but there are also children. You will have Our List and Our History, written by two of the children.

Our history–in case we perish

Six weeks ago the Virus X killed lots and lots of people. We were lucky and we are still here in this small schoolroom. All here but Mr Brown who was brave and took our gun on the second day and he went into the village even though there was only one bullet and the wild dogs were barking and we could hear the bears and we heard one shot and he did not come back and we all decided to stay here until all our food has been eaten.

Six weeks ago the weather was mild and now it is very cold and getting colder and windy and we have no warm clothes, no knives. There is no water from the tap in the small wash-basin and no electricity. There is a fireplace and we have burned an old cupboard to help us keep warm but there are no more cupboards to burn.

This morning a helicopter flew over but did not come back and it is the only helicopter we have seen and no planes and the road is always empty and nothing is outside but the animals.

Our list—what we have after six weeks

- About 100 tins of food.
- About 200 empty tins, plus 200 lids.
- One saw for wood.
- One hacksaw.
- One hammer.
- One tin-opener with sharp point.
- Three large balls of string (thick, medium and thin).
- Ten boxes of matches.
- 50 story books with pictures.
- 50 large sheets of drawing paper, crayons, pens, paints.
- Two buckets of rain-water—one for washing and one for drinking.
- One very large sheet of tarpaulin and some wooden board which we put out of the window to catch rain.
- About 1000 nails (mostly iron) of various sizes in a wooden box.
- One large wooden table.
- Electric wire on the walls, some of it copper wire.
- Six small wooden chairs for children and a large wooden chair for the teacher.
- Six blankets and the remains of cardboard boxes (used for sleeping).
- Two large wooden shelves used for the books.
- Old linoleum about 10 metres square on concrete floor.

36 War canoes

Description A simulation about a tribe which has sighted war canoes in the distance.

Objectives To enhance the skills of creativity, communication, diplomacy, negotiation, planning, presentation and teamwork. There is a hidden agenda in the sense that members of the tribe have their own profiles outlining their thoughts about the situation. It is possible that issues of gender and race might arise.

Time and numbers With small numbers, the event might last for an hour. If there are two or more events run in parallel, more time will be needed in the debriefing for explanation and comments and the event could take up to two hours. The minimum number is probably four. There is no maximum number.

Resources
- Briefing sheet—one copy for each participant.
- Law of the Stick—one copy for each participant.
- Proposals—one copy for each participant.
- Attitude cards—one only for each point of view: Defence, Leisure, Religion and Trade.
- A 'stick' (ruler, twig, tape recorder).
- Scrap paper.

Method
1. Hand out the Briefing sheets and arrange the furniture into groups, depending on the number of participants. With eight participants, there could be two groups of four or one group of eight, with two participants representing each of the four points of view. With seven participants, one point of view could be represented by one participant and the other three points of view by two participants but, in any voting with uneven numbers, the single participant should be entitled to two votes. Set a deadline for the end of the event.
2. Retrieve the Briefing sheets and hand out the Law of the Stick and the Proposals—one of each for each participant.
3. With more than one group, divide the participants at random and place the Attitude cards face down, allowing the participants to pick their own. (Make sure that the number of cards matches the four individuals

or teams. To hand out two Defence cards and no Leisure card could be embarrassing.)
4 Make scrap paper available.

Debriefing

It is a good idea to start with teams reading their Attitude cards. If there was more than one meeting, each meeting (or team) could reveal what happened, including any plans or deals.

Did anyone in any meeting request time out for private talks? What plans were created? Were there any examples of participants using diplomacy or negotiation? How well did the participants accept the situation and create for themselves the sort of thoughts and values of ancient tribespeople? To what extent was the situation similar to present-day issues? The discussion could deal with all skills that might be involved—creativity, communication, diplomacy, negotiation, planning and teamwork.

Briefing This is a simulation about a tribe which has sighted war canoes in the distance. You are a member of the tribe and you will have two public documents—the Law of the Stick, which deals with traditional procedure at meetings of the tribe, plus a list of four proposals which have been put forward for discussion. These four proposals reflect different priorities for the tribe—Defence, Leisure, Religion and Trade. You will have a private document—Attitudes—which gives your initial attitude on these issues.

The first time you speak at the meeting you must set forth the attitude in the best way you can. By the second time you speak you can, if you wish, modify or change your attitude, depending on the views that have been put forward.

At meetings of the tribe no one is leader. Sometimes the people vote on proposals, sometimes no vote is taken.

Do not play-act being a member of a tribe. Simply try to enter the situation of a tribe which has more spare time because of division of labour (specialists, not everyone trying to make everything for themselves). Try to adjust your thinking to tribal thinking and accept tribal values.

Law of the Stick
The Stick of Speech, Wisdom and Respect

The Stick must be passed round.

Only the person holding the Stick can speak.

A person without the Stick must not speak.

The person with the Stick can pass it on without speaking.

A meeting can break up for Rest or Private Talk.

The person holding the Stick must lay it down as a request for Rest or Private Talk.

If the next person does not pick up the Stick the meeting breaks up.

The meeting resumes after twelve waves have washed the sand.

Proposals

Defence

All spare time for the next 12 months be used for defence—building war canoes, making more weapons, building a stockade and training warriors.

Leisure

All spare time for the next six months be used for leisure—building a meeting place, huts for artists, help for sports, dancing, music, poetry, story-telling and philosophy.

Religion

All spare time for the next nine months be used for religion—building a house of the gods and for training religious leaders who will serve the gods and the gods of our tribe will be saved and will prosper.

Trade

All spare time for the next six months be used for trade—building a market, storehouses and for searching for other tribes in order to trade with them.

Attitude: Defence

We are not against trade, religion or leisure. But defence must come first. We have seen war canoes across the sea. If we are attacked, our huts could be burned, our pots broken, our men killed and our women and children taken away. Perhaps the Religious group would support our proposal. They believe that the tribe as a tribe is more important than the individual. If we spend our time on trade, then we would become a ripe plum ready for taking. If we spend the time on leisure, then our minds and bodies would turn towards selfish pleasures and we would become cowards.

Attitude: Leisure

We are not against defence, religion or trade. But leisure must come first. Only in leisure can we enjoy the quality of life. In leisure we become free. We can live rather than slave. We can dance, sing, compete in noble sports and create beauty. The Religious group would use us only to strengthen their own power and the Defence group would breed warriors who would spurn art. Perhaps the Trade group would support our proposal, since art can be a great source of trade, and exploration and peaceful trade can bring forth new art and new beauty and new truth.

Attitude: Religion

We are not against defence, trade or leisure. But religion must come first. The gods are stronger than the tribe. If we fear them and respect them and serve them, then they will aid us in times of trouble. They are stronger than weapons, stronger than riches and stronger than poems. Weapons breed warriors and warriors want to rule. Trade breeds wealth and the wealthy want to rule to preserve their wealth. Perhaps the Leisure group would support our proposal because they believe in beauty and truth and could help us make beautiful a house of the gods, who would then look with favour on our tribe and all who are in it.

Attitude: Trade

We are not against defence, religion or leisure. But trade must come first. Trade is the way towards a better life for ourselves and our children and our children's children. The Religious group would have us all on our knees, in rags, doing nothing but praying and worshipping. The Leisure group would try to keep us in happy poverty. Perhaps the Defence group would support our proposal because we could then afford warriors to keep us safe from thieves, brigands and warlike tribes.

37 Year of the Dove

Description A simulation in which scribes of the Mountains and the Plains meet to exchange information and ideas.

Objectives To enhance the skills of creativity, artistry, communication, diplomacy, negotiation, planning, presentation and teamwork in a situation which might involve aspects of race and gender. There is a hidden agenda in the sense that the people of the Mountains and the Plains each have their own document about their own culture.

Time and numbers With small numbers the event might last for an hour but, with larger numbers, allow up to two hours. The minimum number is probably eight. There is no maximum number.

Resources
- Briefing sheet—one copy for each participant.
- Mountain Council—one copy for each of the Mountain People.
- Circle of the Plains—one copy for each of the people of the Plains.
- Two (or three) rooms are advisable.
- Scrap paper, plus some large sheets and coloured pens.

Method
1. Hand out the Briefing sheets—one copy for each participant. Discuss the facilities, including the locations (preferably in two rooms) of the Mountain people and the Plains people. Set three time-limits—for the start of the joint meeting, for the end of the joint meeting and for the end of the event. Allow sufficient time in the first session for the participants to create their works—drawings, paintings, diagrams, etc.
2. If there are three rooms, one can be the neutral territory for the meeting, otherwise one of the other rooms should be allocated and the furniture in this room made as flexible as possible to allow the participants the opportunity to meet in pairs, small groups or large groups and perhaps flow rather than remain in one place.
3. Retrieve the Briefing sheets. Separate the participants at random into two groups of about equal size and hand out the Mountain Council and Circle of the Plains documents to the respective groups.
4. Make scrap paper available, including some large sheets and coloured pens.

Debriefing

This could start with each side remaining together and passing their private documents to the other side. The debriefing can then develop with participants relating their experiences—of their own community and of the other community. If the participants are used to being in a competitive environment, it might be useful to ask if they obeyed the instructions of their leaders and behaved in peace and friendship or simply tried to prove that 'Our people are the best'. To what extent, if any, did gender and race enter into the considerations? What parallels could be drawn with today's world? The discussion can cover the skills involved—creativity, artistry, communication, diplomacy, negotiation, planning, presentation and teamwork. Did any trade discussions take place? How artistic were the drawings and how effective were the presentations of the cultures?

Briefing

This is a simulation which takes place 2000 ago in ancient Alpha. Scribes of the Mountains and scribes of the Plains meet to exchange information and ideas. In the past there has been very little contact between the two communities, neither community having any real knowledge of the life and culture of the other community.

You are a scribe—a person who writes or draws—and you live with your community either in the Mountains or the Plains.

Both sets of scribes have a private document from their leaders—one from the Mountain Council and the other from the Circle of the Plains. It is about a meeting which is restricted to scribes only. It will take place in the foothills halfway between the two communities and is the first 'official' contact between the two peoples. In honour of the meeting this year has been named Year of the Dove.

In stage one you meet as a community in your homeland, in stage two you are at the joint meeting, and in stage three you are back in your homeland.

Do not play-act. Simply accept your responsibilities and be loyal to your leaders.

MOUNTAIN COUNCIL

We, the Mountain Council, give permission to our Scribes to meet with Scribes from the Plains. We give permission for our Scribes to talk peace, but not to talk war, to talk trade but not to talk enmity.

We remind our Scribes that last winter was so cold we were not able to hunt. But we have good bulls which would help to breed the herds of cattle on the Plains and we have strong timber which we use for our houses and we have our tools and hunting spears.

We give permission to our Scribes to draw and write about our culture—about the way the chairs are arranged at the Council, the totem pole of the Great Hunt, the chants of children as the strongest climbs the Tall Tree, the drawing of the Demon of the Mountains on the North Wall of the Temple of the Strong, of the Wild Strawberry poems written by lovers to their loved ones at the time of the wild strawberries, and of the patterns woven into dresses of women for their wedding day. These, or other drawings or words, will honour the Culture of the Mountains.

CIRCLE OF THE PLAINS

We, the Circle of the Plains, do give our Scribes permission to meet with the Scribes from the Mountains. We ask our Scribes to talk of peace not war, to talk of trade, not enmity.

We remind our Scribes that winter was so bad that the wind did tear down our huts and damage our fruit trees and many of our cattle died. But we have fields for grain and the fruit will grow again.

We give permission to our Scribes to draw and show our culture of the Plains—the drawing of the Circle of the Plains, the chants of the farm people for rain, the flower garlands of the children, the drawing of the Devil Mask of the Lord of the Swamp, the Oath of Friendship of the Runners, the Joy Dances and the Love Rings—poems carved on wooden rings and given at weddings. These, or other drawings and words, will honour the Culture of the Plains.